THE CONSTITUTIONAL GUIDE;

COMPRISING

THE CONSTITUTION

OF

THE UNITED STATES;

WITH

NOTES AND COMMENTARIES

FROM THE WRITINGS OF

JUDGE STORY, CHANCELLOR KENT, JAMES MADISON, AND

OTHER DISTINGUISHED AMERICAN CITIZENS.

COMPILED BY

R. K. MOULTON.

THE LAWBOOK EXCHANGE, LTD.
Clark, New Jersey

ISBN 978-1-58477-754-0 (hardcover)
ISBN 978-1-61619-101-6 (paperback)

Lawbook Exchange edition 2008, 2014

The quality of this reprint is equivalent to the quality of the original work.

THE LAWBOOK EXCHANGE, LTD.
33 Terminal Avenue
Clark, New Jersey 07066-1321

Please see our website for a selection of our other publications and fine facsimile reprints of classic works of legal history:

www.lawbookexchange.com

Library of Congress Cataloging-in-Publication Data

Moulton, R. K.
  The constitutional guide, comprising the Constitution of the United States; with notes and commentaries from the writings of Justice Story, Chancellor Kent, James Madison, and other distinguished American citizens / Moulton, R.K., compiler.
    p. cm.
  Originally published: New York : G. & C. Carvill & Co., 1834.
  Includes bibliographical references and index.
  ISBN-13: 978-1-58477-754-0 (cloth : alk. paper)
  ISBN-10: 1-58477-754-0 (cloth : alk. paper)
  1. Constitutional law--United States. I. Title.
  KF4550.M68 2007
  342.7302--dc22
                        2007026560

Printed in the United States of America on acid-free paper

THE
CONSTITUTIONAL GUIDE;

COMPRISING

THE CONSTITUTION

OF

THE UNITED STATES;

WITH

NOTES AND COMMENTARIES

FROM THE WRITINGS OF

JUDGE STORY, CHANCELLOR KENT, JAMES MADISON, AND

OTHER DISTINGUISHED AMERICAN CITIZENS.

COMPILED BY

R. K. MOULTON.

New-York:

SOLD BY G. & C. CARVILL & CO.; HALSTEAD & VOORHIES;
D. APPLETON & CO.; BETTS & ANSTICE; AND
CHARLES S. FRANCIS.

1834.

Entered according to an Act of Congress, in the year 1834, by R. K. MOULTON, in the Clerk's Office of the Southern District of New-York.

TO

THE PEOPLE OF THE UNITED STATES.

I DEDICATE this small volume to you. With no pretensions to literary distinction, or to a knowledge of the magna charta of our rights and liberties, beyond what ought to be possessed by every free citizen; I aim at nothing but a plain and concise explanation of the fundamental principles of our government. No apology is thought necessary for an undertaking, having for its object a manual upon a subject in which all are directly interested, and in which all equally participate. The people being the only source of legitimate authority, their happiness and prosperity, so far as good government is concerned, depend entirely upon themselves. Should they abuse the trust reposed in them, the sin will lie at their own door. "Who," in the language of the learned Judge Story, " can preserve the rights and liberties of the people, when they shall be abandoned by themselves? Who shall keep watch in the temple, when the watchmen sleep at their posts? Who shall call upon the PEOPLE to redeem their possessions, and revive the republic, when their own hands have deliberately and corruptly surrendered them to the oppressor, or have built the prison or dug the graves of their own friends?"

It is to be hoped that so dark a picture of human corruption, will never be applicable to this republic; still the warning voice of history admonishes us to be on the watch. The stability of our republican institutions must rest upon the virtue, intelligence, and sagacity of the people; to aid in the promotion of these qualities, is the object of this work—how far I shall have succeeded, time must determine. In presenting a commentary on each article, I have freely selected from the writings of Story, Kent Madison, and other distinguished citizens

Finding it indispensable to be as concise as possible, I have, in many cases, for the sake of brevity, given the ideas of the learned commentators, but not precisely in their own language. Other points, proper for discussion, have presented themselves to view, which were but slightly or not at all touched upon by the learned commentators. In such cases, I was obliged to be guided wholly by common sense, and without a chart or compass, launch into an unexplored subject. The capitals, punctuation, and orthography of the Constitution itself, are precisely the same as the original draft, deposited in the office of the Department of State. This being the first edition, it is not to be expected but that errors may have imperceptibly crept into the work—but if any, they are unintentional—and as the compiler expects this production to be a subject of fair criticism, he will feel grateful to any person who shall point out its imperfections.

R. K. MOULTON.

New-York, October, 1834.

CONSTITUTION

OF

THE UNITED STATES.

COPIED FROM, AND COMPARED WITH, THE ROLL IN THE DEPARTMENT OF STATE.

WE the People of the United States, in order to form a more perfect Union, establish Justice, insure domestic Tranquillity, provide for the common defence, promote the general Welfare, and secure the Blessings of Liberty to ourselves and our Posterity, do ordain and establish this Constitution for the United States of America.[1]

ARTICLE I.

SECTION 1. All legislative Powers herein granted shall be vested in a Congress of the United States, which shall consist of a Senate and House of Representatives.[2]

1. This is a better recognition of popular rights, than volumes of those aphorisms, which make a principal figure in several of our State Bills of Rights, and which would sound much better in a treatise of ethics, than in a constitution of government.—*Story's Commentaries on the Constitution, volume* 3, *page* 715.

2. This section involves, as a fundamental rule, the

SECTION 2. The House of Representatives shall be composed of Members chosen every second year by the People of the several States,³ and the Electors in each State shall have the Qualifications requisite for Electors of the most numerous Branch of the State Legislature.

No person shall be a Representative who shall not have attained to the age of twenty-five years, and been seven Years a Citizen of the United States, and who shall not, when elected, be an Inhabitant of that State in which he shall be chosen.⁴

exercise of the legislative power by two distinct and independent branches. Under the confederation, the whole legislative power of the union was vested in a single branch. Limited as was that power, the concentration of it in a single body, was deemed a prominent defect of the confederation.—*Story's Com. vol. 2, p. 26.*

3. The American people, long before the adoption of the Federal Constitution, had enjoyed the privilege of electing, at least, one branch of the legislature, and in some of the colonies, of electing all the branches composing the legislature. This right was familiar to all the colonies, and was held by them in the highest reverence and respect.—*Substance of Story's Com. vol. 2, p. 46-7.*

The "qualifications requisite for Electors" are prescribed in each State by its own Constitution.—*Compiler.*

4. It is obvious, that the inquiry, as to the due qualifications of representatives, like that, as to the due qualifications of electors in a government, is susceptible, in its own nature, of very different answers, according to the habits, institutions, interests, and local peculiarities of different nations. It is a point, upon which we can arrive at no universal rule, that will accommodate itself to the welfare and wants of every people, with the

Representatives and direct Taxes shall be apportioned among the several States which may be included within this Union, according to their respective Numbers,* which shall be determined by adding to the whole number of free Persons, including those bound to Service for a Term of Years, and excluding Indians not taxed, three-fifths of all other Persons.[5] The same proportionate advantages.—*Story's Com. vol. 2, p. 89.*

5. In the convention that framed the constitution, there was a considerable diversity of opinion, as to the most just and equitable method of apportioning representatives.

The scheme, however, of making numbers the basis of the representation of the Union, seems to have obtained more general favour, than any other in the convention, because it had a natural and universal connexion with the rights and liberties of the whole people. It moreover had the recommendation of greater simplicity and uniformity in its operation, and of being less liable to fraud and evasion, than any other which could be devised. But notwithstanding the plausibility of the plan, so far as relates to free population, difficulties of a serious nature arose, as to the slave population. It was finally agreed that slaves should be represented under the mild appellation of " other persons," not as free persons, but only the proportion of three-fifths. The clause was in substance borrowed from the resolve, passed by the continental congress on the 18th of April, 1783, recommending the States to amend the articles of the confederation in such manner, that the national expenses should be defrayed out of a common treasury, " which shall be supplied by the several States, in proportion to the whole number of white, or

---

* The constitutional provision that direct taxes shall be apportioned among the several States according to their respective numbers, to be ascertained by a census, was not intended to restrict the power of imposing direct taxes to States only.—*Loughborough vs. Blake,* 5 *Wheaton,* 319.

actual Enumeration shall be made within three years after the first Meeting of the Congress of the United States, and within every subsequent Term of ten years, in such Manner as they shall by Law direct. The Number of Representatives shall not exceed one for every thirty thousand,* but each State shall have at least one Representative; and until such enumeration shall be made, the State of New-Hampshire shall be entitled to chuse three, Massachusetts eight, Rhode-Island and Providence Plantations one, Connecticut five, New-York

other free inhabitants, of every age, sex, and condition, including those bound to servitude for a term of years, and three-fifths of all other persons, not comprehended in the foregoing description; except Indians not paying taxes, in each State."

In order to reconcile the non-slaving holding States to this provision, another clause was inserted, that direct taxes should be apportioned in the same manner as representatives. This compromise was also made, in order to reconcile the Southern States to other provisions in the constitution, and especially to the power of making commercial regulations by a mere majority, which was thought to peculiarly favour the Northern States.—*Story's Com. v.* 2, *p.* 107. 111, 112, 113.

Although this article prescribes that "representatives and direct taxes shall be apportioned among the several States according to their numbers," still its provisions will not, in all cases, operate according to the exact letter. Suppose for instance, that a state has a population of 70,000, and the ratio of representation be 50,000, such a State would have *only* one representative, but its quota of taxation would be two-fifths more than that of its representation.—*Compiler.*

---

* See Laws U. S. vol. ii, ch. 124; iii. 261; iv. 332. Acts of 17 Congress, 1 session, ch. 10.

six, New-Jersey four, Pennsylvania eight, Delaware one, Maryland six, Virginia ten, North-Carolina five, South-Carolina five, and Georgia three.

When vacancies happen in the Representation from any State, the Executive Authority thereof shall issue Writs of Election to fill such Vacancies.⁶

The House of Representatives shall chuse their Speaker and other Officers; and shall have the sole Power of Impeachment.

SECTION 3. The Senate of the United States shall be composed of two Senators from each State, chosen by the Legislature thereof, for six years; and each Senator shall have one Vote.*⁸

6. Should a member of congress die, resign, or otherwise vacate his seat, before the expiration of the term for which he was chosen, his successor will serve only for the unexpired time of the person whose place he is chosen to supply.—*Compiler.*

7. The power of impeachment, is designed as a method of national inquest into the conduct of public men. Who then can so properly be the inquisitors for the nation, as the representatives of the people themselves?—*Story's Com. v. 2, p.* 171.

8. We will take into view, in the first place, the nature of the representation and vote of the Senate. Each state is entitled to two senators; and each senator to one vote. This, of course, involves, in the very constitution of this branch of the legislature, a perfect equality among all the States without any reference to their respective size, population, wealth, or power. In this respect, there is a marked contrast between the *senate* and the *house of representatives.* In *the latter*, there is a

---

* See art. v, clause 1.

Immediately after they shall be assembled in Consequence of the first Election, they shall be

representation of the people according to the relative population of each state upon a given basis; in the *former, each state in its political capacity*, is represented upon a footing of perfect equality.

It is obvious, that this arrangement could only arise from a compromise between independent States.—*Story's Com. v. 2, p.* 173.

HISTORICAL FACTS IN RELATION TO THE SENATE.

In the convention that framed the Constitution, the small States insisted upon an equality of vote and representation in each branch; and the large States upon a vote in proportion to their relative importance and population. Upon this vital question there was so near a balance of the States, that a Union in any form of government, which provided either for a perfect equality or inequality of the States in both branches of the Legislature, became utterly hopeless. A compromise was, therefore, indispensable, or the convention must be dissolved. The small States at length yielded the point, as to an equality of representation in the house, and acceded to a representation proportionate to the federal numbers; but they insisted upon an equality in the Senate.

The subject was finally referred to a Committee, who reported a scheme, which became, with some amendments, the basis of the representation, as it now stands.—REMARKS.

If the house is to be proportional to the relative *population* of the States, the Senate should be fixed upon an absolute equality, as the representatives of State Sovereignty.

There is so much reason, and justice, and security in such a course, that it can with difficulty be overlooked by those, who sincerely consult the public good, without being biassed by the interests or prejudices of their peculiar local position. The equal vote allowed in the Senate is, in this view, at once a constitutional recognition of the sovereignty remaining in the States, and an instrument for the preservation of it.

divided as equally as may be into three Classes. The Seats of the Senators of the first Class shall be vacated at the Expiration of the second Year, of the second Class at the Expiration of the fourth Year, and of the third Class at the Expiration of the sixth Year, so that one-third may be chosen every second Year;[9] and if vacancies happen by Resignation, or otherwise, during the Recess of the Legislature of any State, the Executive thereof may make temporary appointments until the next Meeting of the Legislature, which shall then fill such Vacancies.[10]

No Person shall be a Senator who shall not have attained to the age of thirty Years,[11] and

Another and most important advantage arising from this ingredient is, the great difference, which it creates in the elements of the two branches of the legislature. It may be safely asserted, that for all the purposes of liberty, and security, and of stable laws, and of solid Institutions, of personal rights, and of the protection of property, a single branch is quite as good as two, if their composition is the same, and their spirits and impulses the same.—*Story's Com. v.* 2, *p.* 173. 175. 178, 179.

9. Here is a clause, which, without impairing the efficiency of the Senate, for the discharge of its high functions, gradually changes its members, and introduces a biennial appeal to the States, which must forever prohibit any permanent combination for sinister purposes.—*Story's Com. v.* 2, *p.* 202.

10. In cases where a member of the Senate by death, resignation, or from any other cause, vacates his seat, his successor is elected only for the unexpired period of the six years for which his predecessor was chosen.— *Compiler.*

11. The age of senators was fixed in the constitution at first by a vote of seven states against four; and finally, by a unanimous vote. Perhaps no one,

been nine Years a Citizen of the United States, and who shall not, when Elected, be an Inhabitant of that State for which he shall be chosen.

The Vice-President of the United States shall be President of the Senate,[12] but shall have no vote, unless they be equally divided.[13]

The Senate shall chuse their other Officers, and also a President pro-tempore, in the absence of the Vice-President,[14] or when he shall exercise the office of President of the United States.

The Senate shall have the sole Power to try all Impeachments: When sitting for that Purpose, they shall be on Oath or Affirmation.[15] When the President of the United

in our day, is disposed to question the propriety of this limitation, and it is, therefore, useless to discuss a point, which is so purely speculative.—*Story's Com. v. 2, p. 205.*

12. The necessity of providing for a case of a vacancy in the office of President doubtless gave rise to the creation of the office of Vice-President.—*Story's Com. vol. 2, p. 209.*

13. The Vice-President does not participate in the debates nor in any of the legislative deliberations of the Senate; instances have however occurred in that body, in which, on giving the casting vote, he has given the reasons for his vote.—*Compiler.*

14. The propriety of intrusting the Senate with the choice of its other officers, and also of a President pro-tempore in the absence of the Vice-President; or when he exercises the office of President, seems never to have been questioned; and indeed is so obvious, that it is wholly unnecessary to vindicate it.—*Story's Com. v. 3, p. 213.*

15. The jurisdiction of impeachment is to be exercised

over offences, which are committed by public men in violation of their public trust and duties.

The convention appears to have been very strongly impressed with the difficulty of constituting a suitable tribunal for the trial of impeachment; and finally came to the result, that the Senate, from the manner in which that body was constituted, was the most fit depository of this exalted trust. In so doing, they had the example before them of several of the best considered State Constitutions; and the example, in some measure, of Great Britain.

The scheme did not entirely escape opposition. Among other objections it was urged,—that the provision confounds the legislative and judiciary authorities in the same body, in violation of the well known maxim which requires a separation of them.

In answer to the objection " that the provision confounds the legislative and judiciary authorities,"—the question is not so much, whether any intermixture is allowable, as whether the intermixture of authority to try impeachments with other functions of the Senate, is salutary and useful. Now, some of these functions constitute a sound reason for the investment of the power in this branch. The offences which the power of impeachment is designed principally to reach, are those of a political, or of a judicial character. They are not those which are within the scope of the ordinary municipal jurisprudence of a country. They are founded on different principles; are governed by different maxims, are directed to different objects, and require different remedies from those, which ordinarily apply to crimes. *In regard to political offences, the selection of the Senators has some positive advantages. In the first place, they may be fairly presumed to have a more enlarged knowledge, than persons in other situations, of political functions, and their difficulties, and embarrassments; of the extent, limits, and variety of executive powers and operations; and of the sources of involuntary error, and undesigned excess, as contra distinguished from those of meditated and violent disregard of duty and right.* On the one hand, this very experience and knowledge will bring them to the trial with a spirit of candour and intelligence, and an ability to comprehend and scrutinize the charges against the accused; and, on the other hand, their connexion with, and dependence on, the States, will make them feel a just regard for the defence of the rights, and the interests of the States and the people. —*Story's Com. v.* 3, *p.* 217. 219, 220, 221.

From the foregoing remarks of the learned commentator, and from the Constitution itself, it is clear that the Senate are constituted, in one capacity, a Court for the trial of impeachments; and in another capacity, a legislative branch of government, co-equal with the House of Representatives, excepting the right to originate bills for raising revenue.

As a legislative branch, they must necessarily be judges and interpreters of the Constitution under which they act, and which they are sworn to support; they moreover, like all other bodies of a similar character, must, from the very nature of their offices, be the sole Judges of the extent and limits of their powers and duties.

In the exercise of their legislative functions, it is the right and duty of the Senate, as a co-ordinate branch of government, not only to create such laws as they may deem conducive to the public good, but also to make such alterations, modifications, and amendments in the existing laws, as experience shall have proved requisite; and in their legislative deliberations, it is not only their right, but in certain cases, it is their duty, to bring into view, the whole operations of the government; including the existing laws, and the conduct of those intrusted with their execution. Nor is that body in any way restrained, except by its own rules, in the freedom of discussion, and in the freedom of legislative action. No matter if what is said or done, in the course of legislation, may incidentally or ultimately affect another department of government, or some officer, intrusted with the execution of the laws, the legislative action of the Senate is subject to no restraint on that account;—the charter under which they act, contemplates that they be guided by no principle, other than a fearless support of the Constitution, and as far as their judgment dictates, the promotion of the general welfare. That the compiler may not be misunderstood, he deems it proper to say that he does not assert that the Senate are subject to no restraint *for what they may have done or accomplished.*

They may pass such a law, as the President may think proper to negative, which of course becomes a dead letter, unless, after reconsideration, the same is passed by a majority of two-thirds of both houses, and even then, it may be set aside by the Supreme Court, should it be in violation of the constitution. In like manner, if they were to make an unlawful requisition upon a government officer, there can be no doubt but the officer would be justifiable in refusing a compliance with such a requisition. It is not, therefore, in the *effect* of laws or resolutions passed by the Senate, that that body is unrestrained, but in the act of *framing laws* or resolutions.

The compiler is led to these remarks from a recent occurrence, in which the President of the United States, in a communication to the Senate, protests against their exercising certain legislative functions, and disputes the right of that body to pass a certain resolution, in relation to his official conduct, upon the ground that he might be impeached for the transaction. The resolution grew out of a report of the Committee on finance in relation to the removal of the public deposites from the United States Bank, and was in the words following: "Resolved that the President, in the late executive proceedings in relation to the public revenue, has assumed to himself authority and power not conferred by the Constitution and laws, but in derogation of both."

This was an act of legislation, confined exclusively to the Senate, and of such a nature, that the President could not be constitutionally required or called upon, as a co-ordinate branch of government, to approve or disapprove. This communication, or protest as it was called, was therefore, in a constitutional point of view, wholly uncalled for. It was, in the view of the compiler, assuming a right, to dictate to the Senate, the extent and limits of their powers and duties: a right, of which, as has been already shown, they are the sole judges: and it requires but little discernment to perceive that if the principle contended for by the President, be correct or even if it be acceded to upon the ground of common courtesy, the great end and aim of legislation, which among other things is " to provide for the common defence and general welfare" can be wholly defeated.*

As for example, the Post-Master General might squander the public moneys upon political favourites. The Secretary, Comptroller, and Register of the Treasury, with the assistance of the Treasurer, might make such disbursements of the public moneys as are unwarranted by law. Collectors of customs might adopt the most unwarrantable, vexatious, and oppressive rules and regulations as to importers; and in fact every officer of the government, from the highest to the lowest, so long as he satisfied the President, might violate the trust reposed in him, and render his office subservient to the will of one man, and to the worst of purposes, without the fear of any check or restraint, except the slow and tedious process of impeachment. No matter what facts might come to the knowledge of the Senate, showing a violation or perversion of the laws by those intrusted with their execution,—no matter whether such violation be wilful, or through an innocently erroneous construction; if the doctrine of the President be correct, the Senate have no right in their legislative capacity to make any report upon the subject, nor to adopt any measures calculated to check the evils known to them, if in thus legislating, they find it necessary, in order to a full and fair exposition of the subject, to mention the improper conduct of any officer of government: because forsooth, for that improper conduct, the officer might be impeached, and, in that event the Senate would be the tribunal to try him: they must therefore remain silent, for the reason that any legislative action upon the subject, mentioning such improper conduct on the part of the officer, would be prejudging

---

* (Here it may be proper to observe that not only the President, "but all officers of the United States who hold their appointment under the national government, with the exception of officers in the army and navy, are liable to impeachment.")

his case, or, as some say, trying and condemning him, without the formality of a charge from the house of representatives, and without a hearing. The people of these United States, it is to be hoped, never can, never will sanction such a political heresy.

Again, should the principle contended for by the President prevail, not only might the disastrous results, as already shown, to the community follow, but the most serious and oppressive consequences might be visited upon meritorious officers. Instances might arise, in which through mistake, but with the best intentions, an officer might put an erroneous construction on some law intrusted to his supervision: in such a case, an explanatory act of Congress, or perhaps a bare resolution of one house, might remedy the error, and at the same time not affect the officer: but if the Senate in the course of their legislative proceedings, have no right to inquire into and report the manner in which laws have been executed (which must necessarily involve the conduct of the officer) the only alternative must be either to suffer the intentions of the law to be defeated, or subject the officer, whose duty it may be to carry it into execution, to an impeachment. Other obstacles, of a serious nature, calculated to militate against important legislation and the faithful execution of the laws, might arise if the Senate were to be thus trammelled; but the mention of them must necessarily be passed over to make room for a few miscellaneous remarks upon the general drift of the President's communication. Among other things, the writer of the protest, evidently intends to convey the idea, and it is generally so received by the people, that the President stands in the same relation to the Senate, that a culprit does to a petit jury—a few remarks will show the fallacy of such a position. By the rules of the common law, every favour, consistent with attaining the ends of public justice, is shown to a culprit. A person may be arraigned on a charge, which, if proven, would deprive him of life, property, or personal liberty. Under such circumstances, the humane principles of the common law, guards the prisoner against every form of the trial, and against every avenue that might have even the appearance of injustice, or a want of fairness.

Impeachment is a proceeding of purely a political nature. It is not designed so much to *punish* an offender, as to secure the state against gross official misdemeanours. It touches neither his person, nor his property, but simply devests him of his political capacity." (See Article 1st, last clause of Section 3d.)

Admitting, however, for the sake of argument, the cases to be analogous, still the principle contained in the protest cannot be sustained. If the Senate had prejudged the case, we must all admit the proper time for the President to make an objection as to the competency of certain Senators, should be on his arraignment for trial. At our courts of Oyer and Terminer forty-eight jurors are usually impanelled. Suppose that a person was committed for murder, and that it should come to his knowledge, that the 48 jurors, had expressed an opinion that he was guilty. No one will pretend that the prisoner would have the right to challenge a juror for the expression of such an opinion before his arraignment.

But it is unnecessary to dwell upon a useless speculation. If it were an original question, that is to say, if a convention were engaged in framing a constitution, these might be proper subjects for discussion—*but our constitution is adopted.* In that instrument, and in most of our State constitutions, the principle is recognised of constituting the Senate not only a legislative branch of government, but also, for the time, a court of impeachment. Numerous legislative acts, similar to that of the Senate might be mentioned.

One, however, will be particularly noticed as exactly an analogous case.

In 1813, President Madison, during the recess of the Senate, appointed and commissioned ministers to negotiate the treaty of Ghent. The Senate, at their next session, entered a protest against such an exercise of power by the executive—declaring that he had exercised a power, not conferred upon him by the constitution.

On a subsequent occasion, (April 20, 1824,) the Senate seem distinctly to have held, that the President could not create the office of minister, and make appointments to such an office during the recess without the consent of the Senate.

States is tried, the Chief Justice shall preside: And no Person shall be convicted without the Concurrence of two thirds of the Members present.

Judgment in Cases of Impeachment shall not extend further than to removal from Office, and disqualification to hold and enjoy any Office of honour, Trust or Profit under the United States:[16] but the Party convicted shall nevertheless be liable and subject to Indictment, Trial, Judgment and Punishment, according to Law.

Mr. Madison, if we are to form our opinion from his general character, was undoubtedly as jealous of his fame, and as tenacious of his official rights, as any one; but we do not learn, that for this legitimate expression of opinion by the Senate, he ever sent to that body any protests or remonstrances. He undoubtedly considered the transaction, and treated it as an honest difference of opinion between him and the Senate. We moreover do not learn that, in private circles, he was ever known to revile and traduce this branch of government.. He treated it with the respect due to its station, and when his time of office had expired, we find that he peaceably retired to private life, with the respect and good wishes of his fellow citizens. And so long as we have a Senate of the United States, it is to be hoped, that there will be a sufficient number in that body, that will so far respect their own rights—and the rights of the people, as to resist any unwarrantable encroachments by the executive.—*Compiler.*

16. Taking this clause in connexion with Art. 2. Sec. 4. and it would seem to follow that the Senate, on conviction were bound, in all cases, to enter a judgment of *removal from office*, though it has a discretion, as to inflicting the punishment of *disqualification.*—*Story's Com. vol. 2, page* 271.

SECTION 4. The Times, Places and Manner of holding Elections for Senators and Representatives, shall be prescribed in each State by the Legislature thereof; but the Congress may at any time by Law make or alter such Regulations, except as to the Places of chusing Senators.[17]

The Congress shall assemble at least once in every Year, and such meeting shall be on the First Monday in December, unless they shall by law appoint a different Day.

SECTION 5. Each House shall be the Judge of the Elections, Returns and Qualifications of its own Members, and a Majority of each shall constitute a Quorum to do Business; but a smaller Number may adjourn from day to day, and may be authorized to compel the attendance of absent Members, in such manner, and under such Penalties as each House may provide.

Each House may determine the Rules of its Proceedings,* punish its Members for disorderly

---

17. The regulation of elections is submitted in the first instance, to the local governments, which, in ordinary cases, and when no improper views prevail, may both conveniently and satisfactorily be by them exercised. But, in extraordinary circumstances, the power is reserved to the National Government; so that it may not be abused, and thus hazard the safety and permanence of the Union.—*Story's Com. v. 2, p.* 281, 282.

---

* To an action of trespass against the Sergeant at Arms of the House of Reprentatives of the U. States for assault and battery and

Behaviour, and, with the Concurrence of two thirds, expel a Member.[18]

Each House shall keep a Journal of its Proceedings, and from time to time publish the same, excepting such Parts as may in their Judgment require Secrecy; and the Yeas and

18. Neither house have definitely decided what constitutes disorderly behaviour, nor for what causes a member may be expelled. In 1797, William Blount was expelled from the Senate by a unanimous vote. The offence charged against him was an attempt to seduce an American agent from his duty. In this case the Senate decided, that the offence, although not punishable by statute, was inconsistent with the duty and trust of a senator. The British Parliament reserve to themselves the right to expel a member whose conduct is such, as, in the judgment of the house unfits him for parliamentary duties.—*Substance of Story's Com. v. 2. p.* 300.

false imprisonment, it is a legal justification and bar to plead that a Congress was held and sitting during the period of the trespasses complained, and that the House of Representatives had resolved that the plaintiff had been guilty of a breach of the privileges of the House, and of a high contempt of the dignity and authority of the same; and had ordered that the Speaker should issue his warrant to the Sergeant at Arms, commanding him to take the plaintiff into custody wherever to be found, and to have him before the said House to answer to the said charge; and that the Speaker did accordingly issue such a warrant, reciting the said resolution and order, and commanding the Sergeant at Arms to take the plaintiff into custody, &c. and deliver the said warrant to the defendant: By virtue of which warrant the defendant arrested the plaintiff, and conveyed him to the bar of the House, where he was heard in his defence touching the matter of said charge, and the examination being adjourned from day to day, and the House having ordered the plaintiff to be detained in custody, he was accordingly detained by the defendant until he was finally adjudged to be guilty and convicted of the charge aforesaid, and ordered to be forthwith brought to the bar and reprimanded by the Speaker, and then discharged from custody, and after being thus reprimanded, was actually discharged from the arrest and custody aforesaid.—*Anderson* vs. *Dunn,* 6 *Wheaton,* 204.

Nays of the Members of either House on any question shall, at the Desire of one fifth of those Present, be entered on the Journal.[19]

Neither House, during the Session of Congress, shall, without the Consent of the other, adjourn for more than three days, nor to any other Place than that in which the two Houses shall be sitting.

SECTION 6. The Senators and Representatives shall receive a Compensation for their Services, to be ascertained by Law, and paid out of the Treasury of the United States. They shall in all cases, except Treason, Felony and Breach of the Peace, be privileged from arrest during their attendance at the Session of their respective Houses, and in going to and returning from the same ; and for any Speech or Debate in either House, they shall not be questioned in any other Place.[20]

19. The object of this clause is to insure publicity to the proceedings of the legislature, and a correspondent responsibility of the members to their constituents. The restriction of Yeas and Nays to one-fifth is, to prevent the too frequent call from mere caprice, &c.—*Substance of Story's Com. vol. 2, p.* 301–3.

20. The privilege of speech and debate, is strictly confined to what may be spoken in legislative proceedings. In Great Britain the courts have decided, that, although a member of parliament is privileged in *debate*, and cannot be questioned respecting it elsewhere, yet, if he *publishes* his speech, and it contains libellous matter, he is liable to an action and prosecution therefor, as in common cases of libel. And the same principle seems applicable to the privilege of debate and speech in Congress.—*Story's Com. vol.* 2, *p.* 329.

No Senator or Representative shall, during the Time for which he was elected, be appointed to any civil office under the Authority of the United States, which shall have been created, or the Emoluments whereof shall have been increased during such time;[21] and no Person holding any office under the United States, shall be a Member of either House during his Continuance in Office.[22]

SECTION 7. All Bills for raising Revenue shall originate in the House of Representatives; but the Senate may propose or concur with the Amendments as on other Bills.

Every Bill which shall have passed the House of Representatives and the Senate, shall, before it become a Law, be presented to the President of the United States; If he approve he shall sign it, but if not he shall return it, with his Objections to that House in which it shall have originated, who shall enter the Objections at large on their Journal, and proceed to reconsider it. If after such Reconsideration two-thirds of that House shall agree to pass the Bill, it shall be sent, together with the

---

21. The reasons for excluding persons from offices, who have been concerned in creating them, or increasing their emoluments, are to take away, as far as possible, any improper bias in the vote of the Representative, and to secure to his constituents some solemn pledge of his disinterestedness.—*Story's Com. v. 2, p.* 331.

22. A person holding an office under the United States may be elected by the people to Congress, but before entering upon its duties, he must resign his office. —*Compiler.*

Objections, to the other House, by which it shall likewise be reconsidered, and if approved by two thirds of that House, it shall become a Law. But in all such Cases the votes of both Houses shall be determined by Yeas and Nays, and the Names of the Persons voting for and against the Bill shall be entered on the Journal of each House respectively. If any Bill shall not be returned by the President within ten Days (Sunday excepted) after it shall have been presented to him, the same shall be a Law, in like manner as if he had signed it, unless the Congress by their Adjournment prevent its Return, in which case it shall not be a Law.[23]

Every Order, Resolution, or Vote to which

---

23. In the convention that framed the constitution, there was a considerable diversity of opinion, in relation to the veto power. Considering however that congress might hastily and unadvisedly pass laws, evidently injurious to the public interest, inconsistent with the public good, or in violation of the Constitution, the convention, after mature deliberation, clothed the President with the unqualified power of negativing a bill, under a firm conviction that it would be exercised only on extraordinary occasions, similar to those mentioned. In support of the measure, and of what would be its probable result, the convention was influenced, in some measure, by the precedent afforded in the English constitution, under which the King had not exercised the veto prerogative since the year 1692. They moreover had the example of the Constitution of the State of New York, and of Massachusetts; the former of which had been in operation for ten, the latter for seven years.

That the exercise of the veto power is, in certain cases, necessary and justifiable will not, it is believed, be denied by any one.

the Concurrence of the Senate and House of Representatives may be necessary (except on a question of Adjournment) shall be presented to the President of the United States; and before the same shall take effect, shall be approved by him, or being disapproved by him, shall be repassed by two thirds of the Senate and House of Representatives, according to the Rules and Limitations prescribed in the Case of a Bill.

SECTION 8. The Congress shall have Power to lay and collect Taxes,* Duties, Imposts and Excises, to Pay the Debts and provide for the common Defence and general Welfare of the United States; but all Duties, Imposts and

Instances might occur, in which laws are passed under great party excitement, or other circumstances not favourable to judicious legislation. In such cases, the exercise of the veto power would often be attended with salutary consequences. But if the President were to veto a law that had been for some time the subject of discussion and approval among a majority of the people, not only in their primary assemblies, but through their representatives, an act of this kind would, in the view of the compiler, be at least a disrespect of the public will, if not a wanton abuse of power.—*Compiler.*

---

* The power of Congress to *lay and collect taxes, duties, &c.* extends to the District of Columbia, and to the territories of the U. States as well as to the States. *Loughborough* vs. *Blake,* 5 *Wheaton,* 318. But Congress are not bound to extend a direct tax to the district and territories. *Id.* 318.

Excises shall be uniform throughout the United States;[24]

24. Query.—Do the words "to lay and collect taxes, duties, imposts and excises," constitute a distinct, substantial power, and the words, "to pay the debts, and provide for the common defence and general welfare of the United States," constitute another distinct and substantial power? or are the latter words connected with the former, so as to contistute a qualification upon them? The grammatical construction would seem to favour the idea that they constitute two distinct substantial powers, and that the verbs " to lay and collect;" are governed by the verb " shall have" expressed and the verb " to pay" governed by the verb "shall have" understood. This is a topic however on which there has been a great diversity of opinion; some insisting upon the meaning warranted by the grammatical construction, others that the words " to pay," &c., are connected with the former, so as to constitute a qualification upon them. Mr. Jefferson in his opinion to Genl. Washington, Feb. 5, 1791, upon the constitutionality of the United States Bank, considers that the words " to pay," &c., are dependent upon the words " lay and collect," and that the whole sentence is tantamount to the following :—" The congress shall have power to lay and collect taxes, duties, imposts and excise, *for the purpose* of paying the debts," &c.

Query 2. Does congress possess the power to encourage domestic manufactures.

A few authorities will be cited.

When the constitution was framed, no one ever imagined, that the power of protection of manufactures was to be taken away from all the States, and yet not delegated to the Union. The very suggestion would of itself have been fatal to the adoption of the constitution.—*Story's Com. v.* 2, *p.* 525.

It is manifest from contemporaneous documents, that one object of the constitution was to encourage manufactures and agriculture by this very use of the power. The terms, then, of the constitution are sufficiently large to embrace the power; the practice of other nations, and especially of Great Britain, and of the American States has been to use it in this manner, and this exercise of it was one of the very grounds, upon which the constitution was urged and vindicated: the argument, then, in its favour would seem to be absolutely irresistible under this aspect. But there are other very weighty considerations, which enforce it.

In the first place, if congress does not possess the power to encourage domestic manufactures by regulations of commerce, the power is annihilated for the whole nation. The states are deprived of it. They have made a voluntary surrender of it; and yet it exists not in the national government.—*Ib. v.* 2, *p.* 526.

Extracts of a letter from Mr. Madison, to Jos. C. Cabell, Esq., dated Sept. 10, 1828, (Niles Register, vol. 35, page 286.)

After giving the views of several states at the adoption of the Federal constitution, all asserting the right and in favour of encouraging manufactures, Mr. Madison says, "But ample evidence may be found elsewhere, that regulations of trade, for the encouragement of manufactures, was considered as within the power to be granted to the new congress, *as well as within* the scope *of the national policy.*

"If congress have not the power, to encourage manufactures, it is annihilated for the nation; a policy without example in any other nation, and within the reason of the solitary one in our own.

"That the encouragement of manufactures was an object of the power to regulate trade, is proved by the use made of the power for that object, in the first session of the first congress under the constitution, when among the members present, were so many who had been members of the federal convention that framed the constitution."

The preamble of the act of congress, alluded to by Mr. Madison, was in these words: "Whereas it is necessary for the support of government, for the discharge of the debts of the United States, *and the encouragement and protection of domestic manufactures*, that duties be laid on goods, wares, and merchandises, imported."

It is worthy of remark, that the act of congress, to which the foregoing is a preamble, was the second act of the first session of the first congress, and was signed by George Washington, July 4th, 1789.

Mr. Madison, in another place, observes, "A further evidence in support of the constitutional power to protect and foster manufactures by regulations of trade, an evidence that ought of itself, to settle the question, is, the uniform and practical sanction given to the power, by the general government, for nearly forty years, with a concurrence of every state government, throughout the same period; and it may be added, through all the vicissitudes of party, which marked the period."

The right of the national government to encourage manufacturers, by the imposition of duties on imported articles, seems to be so clear, as to admit of no doubt, in the minds of reasonable men.

The amount of duties, as well as the general policy of the measure, is a discretionary power, vested in congress. The advocates of free trade insist, that the consumer pays an additional price for an imported article, equal to the amount of duty.

The friends of the protective system contend, that the price of an imported article is not wholly regulated by its cost, charges, and duty; but that it frequently depends upon other circumstances,—such as the probable demand, a scarcity or overstock in market, &c.,—but admitting the principle, contended for by the advocates of free trade, in its fullest extent, as respects articles of wholly foreign growth or manufacture; still the rule is not applicable to such articles as are exclusively grown or manufactured in the United States. As a sound measure of national policy, the advocates of the protective system contend, that productive labour is a source of wealth, and as an elementary principle, applicable to all nations,—that the greater the amount of productive labour in a country, the greater will be the ability to purchase; and consequently, the greater independence, and comforts of the labouring classes of community. That as a general rule, every successfully manufactured article, cherished by means of the protective policy, brings into requisition skill, enterprise, wealth, and the circulation of money, that would otherwise, in a great measure, remain dormant.

They also contend that it essentially aids the agricultural and farming interest, by creating a home market for grain, and other products of the soil, and at the same time furnishes the farmer, in exchange for his commodity, manufactured articles at a reduced price. The most powerful reason, however, they say, that can be urged in favour of the measure, is, the more equal distribution of wealth, and the comforts of life, which is effected by the increased demand for labour, and its consequent increased value,—that labour, under the protective system, has fully maintained its former price, whilst articles of clothing, particularly of cotton fabrics, are not more than half what they were before the protective policy was brought into successful operation. It requires but a slight knowledge and observation of the human character to discern, that a general diffusion of knowledge, and, as far as practicable, an equal distribution of the comforts of life, are the greatest bulwarks and preservations of a republican government; and that self-interest alone, ought to prompt the rich, to favour such a measure. It is urged by some, that although American manufactures enhance the wealth, and add to the comforts of all concerned in them, still the *consumer may be indirectly taxed*, (none it is believed positively assert that they are) by paying a higher price for an article of domestic manufacture, than for an imported fabric of the like kind. The answer to that is, that *facts* are better evidence than *theory*,—that scarcely a single article, of *American manufacture* —brought into use by means of the protective system, but that is sold at a lower price than a like article formerly was, when imported,—and that a great many articles, affording the manufacturer a reasonable profit, can be furnished the community, at a price, below that which would be the duty on a like article, if imported,—and that particularly, in the article of certain cotton fabrics, which for years have been protected, by a duty, tantamount to a prohibition of the foreign article, the American manufacturer can compete, in a foreign market, with any nation in the world. The same with certain species of glass-ware, and other articles. It is further said, that a **protective tariff does not increase the quantity of** productive labour of the country, but barely diverts it from one channel to another, that is—from commerce to manufactures. In answer to this, it is said, let any one make a calculation of the difference of labour, in manufacturing or importing a hundred yards of cloth, and it will be found that the former will greatly exceed the latter. The advocates of the protective policy moreover contend, that its object is, to *increase*, rather than *diminish* our commerce,—that the interchange of commodities, by water, between New-York and New-Orleans, is as much commerce, as between New-York and Liverpool: and that during the operation of the tariff, our coasting trade has increased in a much greater ratio than at any former period of our government; and at the same time, our foreign trade has not diminished. They moreover assert that the importation of the material necessary to manufacture a yard of broad cloth, requires more shipping, than the cloth in a manufactured state. If then, as the question is often asked, the United States can manufacture as well and as cheap as any other nation, what necessity is there of a high protecting duty?

The answer given is, that by a high protecting duty, the market is secured to the American manufacturer, to the exclusion of the foreign. This creates a confidence in the capitalist, and induces him to vest his funds in an undertaking, which he would otherwise avoid, and in which he comes in competition with none but his own countrymen. This home competition, as has been proved by experience, is sufficient to satisfy all the wants of the community, and, at a reasonable price.

The subject of domestic manufactures, engaged the attention of the wisest and best men, at the incipient stages of our government. It is a topic that deeply concerns the American people, and is

To borrow Money on the credit of the United States;

To regulate Commerce with foreign Nations,[25] and among the several States,[26] and with the Indian Tribes;[27]

respectfully recommended to their serious consideration.—*Compiler.*

25. The want of this power (to regulate commerce) was one of the leading defects of the confederation; and probably, as much as any one cause, conduced to the establishment of the constitution.—*Story's Com. v.* 2, *p.* 504.

In regard to foreign nations, it is universally admitted, that the words, (to regulate commerce with foreign nations) comprehend every species of commercial intercourse. No sort of trade or intercourse can be carried on between this country and another, to which it does not extend.

26. Commerce among the states, means commerce, which concerns more states than one.

The completely internal commerce of a state may be properly considered, as reserved to the state itself.—*Story's Com. v.* 2, *p.* 510.

27. The power given to congress to regulate commerce with the Indian tribes, extends equally to the tribes living *within* or *without* the boundaries of *particular* states; and within or without the territorial limits of the United States.

It has lately been made a question, whether an Indian tribe, situated within the territorial boundaries of a state, but exercising the powers of government, and national sovereignty, under the guaranty of the general government, is a foreign state in the sense of the constitution, and as such, entitled to sue in the Courts of the United States. Upon solemn argument, it has been held, that such a tribe

To establish an uniform Rule of Naturalization,[28] and uniform laws on the subject of * Bankruptcies [29] throughout the United States;

is to be deemed politically a state; that is, a distinct political society, capable of self-government; but it is not to be deemed a *foreign state*, in the sense of the constitution. It is rather a domestic dependent nation. Such a tribe may properly be deemed in a state of pupillage, and its relation to the United States, resembles that of a ward or a guardian.—*Story's Com. v. 2, p.* 542.

Mr. Jefferson's opinion was, that the United States had no more than a right of preemption of the Indian lands, not amounting to any dominion, or jurisdiction, or permanent authority whatever; and that the Indians possessed a full, undivided, and independent sovereignty.—*Jefferson's Correspondence, v.* 4, *p.* 478.

28. There is great wisdom, in confiding to the national government the power to establish a uniform rule of naturalization throughout the United States. It is of the deepest interest to the whole Union to know, who are entitled to enjoy the rights of citizens in each State, since they thereby, in effect, become entitled to the rights of citizens in all the States.—*Story's Com. v.* 3, *p.* 2.

29. It has been strenuously maintained by some learned minds, that the power in congress "to esta-

---

* Since the adoption of the Constitution of the U. States, a State has authority to pass a bankrupt law, provided such law does not impair the obligation of contracts within the meaning of the Constitution, Art. 1, sec. 10, and provided there be no act of Congress in force to establish a uniform system of bankruptcy conflicting with such law. *Sturgess* vs. *Crowningshield,* 4 *Wheaton,* 122. 192.

See Laws U. S. vol. ii, ch. 368, sec. 2; iii, 66; iii, 158.

blish uniform laws on the subject of bankruptcy," *is exclusive* of that of the State; and whether exerted or not, it supersedes state legislation. On the other hand, it has been maintained, that the power in congress *is not exclusive;* that when congress has acted upon the subject, to the extent of the national legislation the power of the states is controlled and limited; but when *unexerted*, the states are at liberty to exercise the power in its full extent, unless so far as they are controlled by other constitutional provisions. And this latter opinion is now firmly established by judicial decisions.— *Story's Com. v. 3, p.* 14.

What laws are to be deemed bankrupt laws within the meaning of the constitution has been a matter of much forensic discussion and argument. Attempts have been made to distinguish between *bankrupt* laws, and *insolvent* laws. For example, it has been said, that laws, which merely liberate the *person* of the debtor, *are insolvent laws*, and those, which *discharge a contract, are bankrupt laws.* But it would be very difficult to sustain this distinction by any uniformity of laws at home or abroad. In some of the states, laws, known as insolvent laws, discharge the *person only;* in others, they discharge the *contract.—Ib.* 10.

It may be stated, that the general object of all bankrupt and insolvent laws is, on the one hand, to secure to creditors an appropriation of the property of their debtors *pro tanto* to the discharge of their debts, whenever the latter are unable to discharge the whole amount; and, on the other hand, to relieve unfortunate and honest debtors from perpetual bondage to their creditors, either in the shape of *unlimited* imprisonment to coerce payment of their debts, or of an absolute right to appropriate and monopolize all their future earnings. The latter course obviously destroys all en-

To coin Money, regulate the Value thereof, and of foreign coin, and fix the Standard of Weights and Measures;[30]

couragement to industry and enterprise on the part of the unfortunate debtor, by taking from him all the just rewards of his labour, and leaving him a miserable pittance, dependent upon the bounty or forbearance of his creditors. The former is, if possible, more harsh, severe, and indefensible. It makes poverty and misfortune, (in themselves sufficiently heavy burthens) the subject or the occasion of penalties and punishments. *Imprisonment*, as a civil remedy, admits of no defence, *except as it is used to coerce fraudulent debtors to yield up their present property to their creditors, in discharge of their engagements.* But when the debtors have no property, or have yielded up the whole to their creditors, to allow the *latter*, at their mere pleasure, to imprison them, *is a refinement in cruelty, and an indulgence of private passions, which could hardly find apology in an* enlightened despotism; and *are utterly at war with all the rights and duties of free government.—Ib.* 4, 5.

30. The only question, which could properly arise under our political institutions, is, whether " the power to coin money, regulate the value thereof, and of foreign coin," should be confided to the *national* or to the *state* government. It is manifest, that the former could alone give it complete effect, and secure a wholesome and uniform currency throughout the Union. The varying standards and regulations of the different states would introduce infinite embarrassments and vexations in the course of trade.

The floods of depreciated paper money, with which most of the states of the Union, during the last war, as well as the revolutionary war with England, were inundated, to the dismay of the traveller, and the ruin of commerce, afford a lively proof of the mischiefs of a currency exclusively under the control of the states.

During the late war with Great Britain, (1812 to 1814) in consequence of the Banks of the middle, and southern, and western states having suspended specie payments for their bank notes, they depreciated as low as 25 per cent. discount from their nominal value. The duties on the imports were, however, paid and received in the local currency; and the consequence was, that goods imported to Baltimore paid 20 per cent. less duty, than the same goods paid, when imported into Boston. This was a plain, practical violation of the provision of the constitution, that all duties, imports and excises shall be *uniform*.

The states cannot coin money. Can they, then, coin that, which becomes the actual and almost universal substitute for money? Is not the right of issuing paper, intended for circulation in the place, and as the representative of metallic currency, derived merely from the power of coining and regulating the metallic currency? Could congress, if it did not possess the power of coining money and regulating the value of foreign coins, create a bank with the power to circulate bills? It would be difficult to make it out. Where, then, do the states, to whom all control over the metallic currency is altogether prohibited, obtain this power? It is a clear indication of the intent of the constitution to restrain the states, as well from *establishing a paper circulation* as from interfering with *the metallic circulation.* Banks have been created by states with no capital whatever, their notes being put in circulation simply on the credit of the state.

To provide for the Punishment of counterfeiting the Securities and current Coin of the United States;[31]

To establish Post Offices and Post Roads;[32]

What are the issues of such banks, but bills of credit *issued by the state?*

But whatever may be the force of this reasoning, it is probably too late to correct the error, if error there be, in the assumption of this power by the states, since it has an inveterate practice in its favour through a very long period, and indeed, ever since the adoption of the constitution.

The other power " to fix the standard of weights and measures," was, doubtless, given from like motives of public policy, for the sake of uniformity, and the convenience of commerce.

Until congress however shall fix a standard, the understanding seems to be, that the states possess the power to fix their own weights and measures.—*Story's Com.* v. 3, p. 18, 19, 20.

31. This power would naturally flow, as an incident from the antecedent powers to borrow money, and regulate the coinage; and, indeed, without it, those powers would be without any adequate sanction.—*Story's Com.* v. 3, p. 21.

32. Upon the construction of this clause of the constitution, two opposite opinions have been expressed. One maintains, that the power to establish post-offices and post-roads can intend no more, than the power to direct, where post-offices shall be kept, and on what roads the mails shall be carried. Or, as it has been on other occasions expressed, the power to establish post-roads, is a power to designate, or point out, what roads shall be mail-roads, and the right of passage or way along them, when so designated.

To promote the Progress of Science and useful Arts, by securing for limited Times to Au-

The other maintains, that although these modes of exercising the power are perfectly constitutional; yet they are not the whole of the power, and do not exhaust it. On the contrary, the power comprehends the right to *make* or *construct* any roads, which congress may deem proper for the conveyance of the mail, and to keep them in due repair for such purpose.

The grounds of the former opinion seem to be as follows :—The power given under the confederation never practically received any other construction. Congress never undertook to make any roads, but merely designated those existing roads, on which the mail should pass. At the adoption of the constitution, there is not the slightest evidence, that a different arrangement, as to the limits of the power was contemplated.

In support of the latter opinion it is urged, that "there is a great difference between the *policy* of exercising a power, and the *right* of exercising it. Suppose the state roads do not furnish, (as in point of fact, they did not at the time of the adoption of the constitution, and as hereafter, for many exigencies of the government, in times of war and otherwise, they may not,) suitable routes for the mails, what is then to be done? Is the power of the general government to be paralyzed? Suppose a mail-road was out of repair and founderous, cannot congress authorize the repair of it? If they can, why then not make it originally? Is the one more a means to an end, than the other? If not, then the power to carry the mails may be *obstructed*; nay, may be *annihilated* by the neglect of a state.—*Story's Com. v.* 3, *p.* 26, 27. 41.

thors and Inventors the exclusive Right to their respective Writings and Discoveries ;[33]

To constitute Tribunals inferior to the Supreme Court ;[34]

To define and punish Piracies and Felonies committed on the high Seas, and Offences against the Law of Nations ;*

33. This power did not exist under the confederation: and its utility does not seem to have been questioned by the framers of the constitution.

The power, in its terms, is confined to *authors* and *inventors;* and cannot be extended to the introducers of any new works or inventions. This has been thought by some persons of high distinction, to be a defect in the constitution. But, perhaps the policy of further extending the right is questionable; and, at all events, the restriction has not hitherto operated as any discouragement of science or the arts.—*Story's Com. v.* 3. *p.* 49.

It has been doubted, whether congress has the authority to decide the fact, that a person is an author or inventor in the sense of the constitution, so as to preclude that question from judicial inquiry.

But, at any rate, there does not seem to be the same difficulty in affirming, that, as the powers of congress extends only to authors and inventors, a state may grant an exclusive right to the possessor or introducer of an art or invention, who does not claim to be an inventor, but has merely introduced it from abroad.—*Livingston* v. *Van Ingen,* 9 *Johns. R.* 507.

34. [See remarks under the third article of the constitution.]

---

* The act of the 3d March, 1819, ch. 76, sec. 5, referring to the law of nations for a definition of the crime of piracy, is a constitutional

To declare War, grant Letters of Marque and Reprisal, and make Rules concerning Captures on Land and Water;[35]

35. That such a power (to declare war, &c.) ought to exist in the national government, no one will deny, who believes, that it ought to have any powers whatsoever, either for offence or defence, for the common good, or for the common protection. The power could not be left without extreme mischief, if not absolute ruin, to the separate authority of the several states; for then it would be at the option of any one to involve the whole in the calamities and burthens of warfare.

The power to declare war, may be exercised by congress, not only by authorizing general hostilities, in which case the general laws of war apply to our situation; but by partial hostilities, in which case, the laws of war, so far as they actually apply to our situation, are to be observed.

The power to declare war would of itself carry the incidental power to grant letters of marque and reprisal, and make rules concerning captures. But the express power to "grant letters of marque and reprisal" may not have been thought wholly unnecessary, because it is often a measure of peace, to prevent the necessity of a resort to war. Thus, individuals of a nation sometimes suffer from the

---

exercise of the power of Congress to define and punish that crime. *United States* vs. *Smith*, 5 *Wheaton*, 153, 157.

Congress have power to provide for the punishment of offences committed by persons on board a ship of war of the United States, wherever that ship may lie: But Congress have not exercised that power in the case of a ship lying in the waters of the United States, the words within fort, arsenal, dock-yard, magazine, or in *any other place or district of country under the sole and exclusive jurisdiction of the United States*, in the third section of the act of 1790, ch. 9, not extending to a ship of war, but only to objects in their nature, fixed and territorial. *The United States* vs. *Bevans*, 3 *Wheaton*, 890.

To raise and support Armies, but no Appropriation of Money to that Use shall be for a longer Term than two Years;[36]

To provide and maintain a Navy;[37]

To make Rules for the Government and Regulation of the land and naval Forces;[38]

depredations of foreign potentates; and yet, it may not be deemed either expedient or necessary to redress such grievances by a general declaration of war. Under such circumstances, the law of nations authorizes the sovereign of the injured individual to grant him this mode of redress, whenever justice is denied to him by the state, to which the party, who has done the injury belongs. In this case, the letters of marque and reprisal, (words used as synonomous, the latter (reprisal) signifying, a taking in return, the former, (letters of marque) the passing the frontiers in order to such taking) contain an authority to seize the bodies or goods of the subjects of the offending state, wherever they may be found, until satisfaction is made for the injury.—*Story's Com. v. 3, p. 59. 62, 63.*

36. The power to raise armies is an indispensable incident to the power to declare war.—*Story's Com. v. 3, p. 64.*

37. In the convention that framed the constitution, the propriety of granting this power, seems not to have been questioned.

The necessity of a navy for the protection of commerce and navigation, was not only admitted, but made a strong ground for the grant of the power.—*Story's Com. v. 3, p. 76, 77.*

38. This is a natural incident to the preceding powers to make war, to raise armies, and to provide and maintain a navy.—*Story's Com. v. 3, p. 79.*

To provide for calling forth the Militia to execute the Laws of the Union, suppress Insurrections and repel Invasions ;[30]

39. Congress in 1795, (see act of 1795, ch. 101) in pursuance of this authority, and to give it a practical operation, provided by law, "that whenever the United States shall be invaded, or be in imminent danger of invasion, from any foreign nation or Indian tribe, it shall be lawful for the President of the United States to call forth such number of the militia of the state, or states, most convenient to the place of danger, or scene of action, as he may judge necessary to repel such invasion. and to issue his orders for that purpose, to such officer or officers of the militia, as he shall think proper." The constitutionality of this act has not been questioned, although it provides for calling forth the militia, not only in cases of invasion, but in imminent danger of invasion; for the power to repel invasions, must include the power to provide against any attempt and danger of invasion, as the necessary proper means to effectuate the object.

By whom is the exigency (the *casus fœderis*, if one may say so,) to be decided? Is the President the sole and exclusive judge, whether the exigency has arisen, or is it to be considered, as an open question, which every officer, to whom the orders of the President are addressed, may decide for himself, and equally open to be contested by every militia-man, who shall refuse to obey the orders of the President?

At a very recent period, the question came before the Supreme Court of the United States for a judicial decision, and it was then unanimously determined, that the authority to decide, whether the exigency has arisen, belongs exclusively to the President; and that his decision is conclusive upon

To provide for organizing, arming, and disciplining the Militia, and for governing such Part of them as may be employed in the Service of the United States, reserving to the States respectively, the Appointment of the Officers,⁴⁰ and the Authority of training the Militia according to the discipline prescribed by Congress ;*

To exercise exclusive Legislation in all Cases whatsoever, over such District (not exceeding ten Miles square) as may, by cession of particular States, and the Acceptance of Congress, become the Seat of the Government of all other persons.—*Story's Com. v.* 3, *p.* 88, 89, 90, 91.

40. To bring the militia within the meaning of being in actual service, there must be an obedience to the call, and some acts of organization, mustering, rendezvous, or marching, done in obedience to the call, in the public service.

It has been a question, whether the militia, called into the actual service of the United States, are to be governed and commanded by any officer, but of the same militia, except the President of the United States; in other words, whether the President can delegate any other officer of the regular army, of equal or superior rank, to command the militia in his absence. This question has never been settled by a definitive judgment of any tribunal competent to decide it.—*Story's Com. v.* 3, *p.* 94, 95.

---

* Vide Amendments, art. 2.

the United States,*⁴¹ and to exercise like Authority over all Places purchased by the Con-

41. The indispensable necessity of complete and exclusive power, on the part of congress, at the seat of government, carries its own evidence with it. It is not improbable, that an occurrence, at the very close of the revolutionary war, had a great effect in introducing this provision into the constitution. At the period alluded to, the congress, then sitting at Philadelphia, was surrounded and insulted by a small, but insolent body of mutineers of the continental army. Congress applied to the executive authority of Pennsylvania for defence; but, under the ill conceived constitution of the state at that time, the executive power was vested in a council, consisting of thirteen members; and they possessed, or exhibited so little energy, and such apparent intimidation, that congress indignantly removed to New-Jersey, whose inhabitants welcomed them with promises of defending them. Congress remained for some time at Princeton without being again insulted, till, for the sake of greater convenience, they adjourned to Annapolis. The general dissatisfaction with the proceedings of Pennsylvania, *and the degrading spectacle of a fugitive congress,* were sufficiently striking to produce this remedy.— *Story's Com. v.* 3, *p.* 97, 98.

The other part of the power, giving exclusive legislation over places ceded for the erection of

---

* Congress has authority to impose a direct tax on the District of Columbia, in proportion to the census directed to be taken by the Constitution. *Loughborovgh* vs. *Blake,* 5 *Wheaton,* 317.

But Congress are not bound to extend a direct tax to the district and territories. *Id.* 322.

The power of Congress to exercise exclusive jurisdiction in all cases whatsoever within the District of Columbia, includes the power of taxing it. *Id.* 324.

sent of the Legislature of the State in which the same shall be, for the Erection of Forts, Magazines, Arsenals, dock-yards, and other needful Buildings;—And

To make all Laws which shall be necessary and proper for carrying into Execution the foregoing Powers, and all other Powers vested by this Constitution in the Government of the United States,[42] or in any Department or officer thereof.*

forts, magazines, &c., seems still more necessary for the public convenience and safety. The public money expended on such places, and the public property deposited in them, and the nature of the military duties which may be required there, all demand, that they should be exempted from state authority. A great variety of cessions have been made by the states under this power. And generally there has been a reservation of the right to serve all state process, civil and criminal, upon persons found therein.—*Story's Com. v.* 3, *p.* 101.

42. Few powers of the government were, at the time of the adoption of the constitution, assailed with more severe invective, and more

---

* Whenever the terms in which a power is granted by the Constitution to Congress, or whenever the nature of the power itself requires that it should be exercised exclusively by Congress, the subject is as completely taken away from the State Legislatures as if they had been expressly forbidden to act on it. *Sturges vs. Crowningshield,* 4 *Wheaton,* 193.

Congress has power to incorporate a bank. *McCulloch vs. State of Maryland,* 4 *Wheaton,* 316.

The power of establishing a corporation is not a distinct sovereign power or end of government, but only the means of carrying into effect other powers which are sovereign. Whenever it becomes an appropriate means of exercising any of the powers given by the Constitution to the government of the Union, it may be exercised by that government. *Id.* '411. 421.

declamatory intemperance, than this. And it has ever since been made a theme of constant attack, and extravagant jealousy. Yet it is difficult to perceive the grounds, upon which it can be maintained, or the logic by which it can be reasoned out. It is only declaratory of a truth, which would have resulted by necessary and unavoidable implication from the very act of establishing the national government, and vesting it with certain powers. What is a power but the ability or faculty of doing a thing? What is the ability to do a thing, but the power of employing the *means* necessary to its execution?—*Story's Com. b.* 3, *p.* 109.

If a certain means to carry into effect any of the powers expressly given by the Constitution to the government of the Union, be an appropriate measure, not prohibited by the Constitution, the degree of its necessity is a question of legislative discretion, not of judicial cognizance. *Id.* 421.

The act of the 19th April, 1816, ch. 44, to incorporate the subscribers to the Bank of the United States, is a law made in pursuance of the Constitution. *Id.* 424.

The Bank of the United States has constitutionally a right to establish its branches or offices of discount and deposit within any State, *Id.* 424.

There is nothing in the Constitution of the United States similar to the articles of confederation, which excludes incidental or implied powers. *Id.* 403.

If the *end* be legitimate and within the scope of the Constitution, all the *means* which are appropriate, which are plainly adapted to that end, and which are not prohibited, may constitutionally be employed to carry it into effect. *Id.* 421.

The powers granted to Congress are not exclusive of similar powers existing in the States, unless where the Constitution has expressly in terms given an exclusive power to Congress, or the exercise of a like power is prohibited to the States, or there is a direct repugnancy or incompatibility in the exercise of it by the States. *Houston* vs. *Moore*, 5 *Wheaton*, 49.

The example of the first class is to be found in the exclusive legislation delegated to Congress over places purchased by the consent of the Legislature of the State in which the same shall be for forts, arsenals, dock-yards, &c. Of the second class, the prohibition of a State to coin money or emit bills of credit. Of the third class, the power to establish a uniform rule of naturalization, and the delegation of admiralty and maritime jurisdiction. *Id.* 49.

The plain import of this clause is, that congress shall have all the *incidental and instrumental powers*, necessary and proper to carry into execution, all the *express powers*. It neither enlarges any power specifically granted; nor is it a grant of any new power to congress.—*Story's Com. v.* 3, *p.* 113.

Whenever, therefore, a question arises concerning the constitutionality of a particular power, the first question is, whether the power be *expressed* in the constitution. If it be, the question is decided. If it be not *expressed*, the next inquiry must be, whether it is properly an incident to an express power, and necessary to its execution. If it be, then it may be exercised by congress. If not, congress cannot exercise it.—*Story's Com. v.* 3, *p.* 114.

The *expediency* of exercising a particular power at a particular time must, indeed, depend on circumstances; but the constitutional right of exercising it must be uniform and invariable; the same to-day, as to-morrow.—*Story's Com. v.* 3, *p.* 117.

In all other classes of cases the States retain concurrent authority with Congress. *Id.* 48.

But in cases of concurrent authority, where the laws of the States and of the Union are in direct and manifest collision on the same subject; those of the Union being the supreme law of the land, are of paramount authority, and the State so far, and so far only as such incompatibility exists, must necessarily yield. *Id.* 49.

The State within which a branch of the United States Bank may be established, cannot without violating the Constitution tax that branch. *McCulloch* vs. *State of Maryland,* 4 *Wheaton,* 425.

The State Governments have no right to tax any of the constitutional means employed by the Government of the Union to execute its constitutional powers. *Id.* 427.

The States have no power by taxation, or otherwise to retard, impede, burden, or in any manner control the operation of the constitutional laws enacted by Congress, to carry into effect the powers vested in the National Government. *Id.* 436.

This principle does not extend to a tax paid by the real property of the Bank of the United States, in common with the other real property in a particular State, nor to a tax imposed on the proprietary which the citizens of that State may hold in common with the other property of the same description throughout the State. *Id,* 436.

Neither can the *degree*, in which a measure is necessary, ever be a test of the *legal right* to adopt it. That must be a matter of opinion, (upon which different men, and different bodies may form opposite judgments,) and can only be a test of expediency. If the legislature possesses a right of choice as to the means, who can limit that choice? Who is appointed an umpire, or arbiter in cases, where a discretion is confided to a government? The very idea of such a controlling authority in the exercise of its powers is a virtual denial of the supremacy of the government in regard to its powers. It repeals the supremacy of the national government, proclaimed in the constitution.—*Story's Com. v. 3, p.* 117, 118.

Upon the whole, the result of the most careful examination of this clause is, that if it does not enlarge, it cannot be construed to restrain the powers of congress, or to impair the right of the legislature to exercise its best judgment, in the selection of measures to carry into execution the constitutional powers of the government.—*Story's Com. v. 3, p.* 123.

And not only may implied powers, but implied exemptions from state authority, exist, although not expressly provided for by law. The collectors of the revenue, the carriers of the mail, the mint establishment, and all those institutions, which are public in their nature, are examples in point. It has never been doubted, that all, who are employed in them, are protected, while in the line of their duty, from state control; and yet this protection is not expressed in any act of congress.—*Story's Com. v. 3, p.* 125.

Another question, which has for a long time agitated the public councils of the nation, is, as to the authority of congress to make roads, canals, and other internal improvements.—*Story's Com. v. 3, p.* 149.

The doctrine which has generally been sanctioned, by the actual practice of the government, is, that congress may appropriate money, not only to clear obstructions to navigable rivers; to improve harbours; to build breakwaters; to assist navigation; to erect forts, light-houses, and piers; and for other purposes allied to some of the enumerated powers; *but may also appropriate it in aid of canals, roads, and other institutions of a similar nature, existing under state authority.* The only limitations upon the power are those prescribed by the terms of the constitution, that the objects *shall be for the common defence or the general welfare of the Union.*—*Story's Com. v* 3, *p.* 149, 150.

The true test is, whether the object be of a *local* character, and *local* use; or whether it be of *general benefit* to the states. If it be purely *local*, congress cannot constitutionally appropriate money for the object. But, if the benefit be *general*, it matters not, whether in point of locality it be in one state, or several; whether it be of large, or small extent, its nature and character determine the right, and congress may appropriate money in aid of it; for it is then in a just sense for the general welfare.

Although a state cannot prevent repairs by the United States on a road used by government, or authorize any obstructions to the same, or in anywise interfere with, or obstruct the legitimate purposes of the general government, still the state does not wholly part with its sovereignty, for it can lawfully punish all crimes and offences committed against its laws.—*Compiler.*

The power to regulate commerce cannot include a power to construct roads and canals.— *Compiler.*

Embargo and Purchase of Foreign Territory.

The most remarkable powers, which have been exercised by the government, as auxiliary and implied powers, and which, if any, go to the utmost verge of liberal construction, are the laying of an unlimited embargo in 1807, and the purchase of Louisiana in 1803, and its subsequent admission into the Union as a state. These measures were brought forward, and supported, and carried by the known and avowed friends of a strict construction of the constitution; and they were justified, at the time, and can be now justified only upon the doctrines of those, who support a liberal construction of the constitution.

In regard to the acquisition of Louisiana; the treaty of 1803 contains a cession of the whole of that vast territory by France to the United States, for a sum exceeding eleven millions of dollars.

There is no pretence, that the purchase, or cession of any foreign territory is neither any of the powers expressly enumerated in the constitution.

If no appropriation of money can be made, except for cases within the enumerated powers, (and this clearly is not one,) how can the enormous sum of eleven millions be justified for this object.

In short there is no possibility of defending the constitutionality of this measure, but upon the principles of the liberal construction, which has been, upon other occasions, so earnestly resisted. The more recent acquisition of Florida, which has been universally approved, or acquiesced in by all the states, can be maintained only on the same principles.—*Story's Com. v.* 3, *p.* 158, 159, 160.

Embargoes.

The other instance of any extraordinary application of the implied powers of the government, is the embargo law in the year 1807, by the special recommendation of President Jefferson.

It (the embargo law) was explicitly stated " to be a measure of precaution called for the occasion ;" and "neither hostile in its character, nor as justifying, or inciting, or leading to hostility with any nation whatever."—*Vide Mr. Madison's Letter to Mr. Pinckney, 7 Wait's State Papers,* 25.

It was in no sense then a war measure. It was in its terms, unlimited in duration, and could be removed only by a subsequent act of congress.

No one can reasonably doubt, that the laying of an embargo, suspending commerce for a limited period, is within the scope of the constitution. But the question of difficulty was, whether congress, under the power to regulate commerce with foreign nations, could constitutionally suspend and interdict it wholly for an unlimited period, that is, by a permanent act, having no limitation as to duration, either of the act, or of the embargo. It was seriously controverted, and its constitutionality denied in the Eastern states of the Union during its existence. An appeal was made to the judiciary upon the question; and it having been settled to be constitutional by that department of the government, the decision was acquiesced in; though the measure bore with most unexampled severity upon the Eastern states, and its ruinous effects can still be traced along their extensive seaboard.

Non-intercourse and embargo laws are within the range of legislative discretion; and if congress have the power, for purpose of safety, of preparation, or counteraction, to suspend commercial intercourse with foreign nations, they are not limited

SECTION 9. The Migration or Importation of such Persons as any of the States now existing shall think proper to admit, shall not be prohibited by the Congress prior to the year one thousand eight hundred and eight, but a Tax or duty may be imposed on such importation, not exceeding ten dollars for each Person.[43]

as to the duration, any more, than as to the manner and extent of the measure.

At the present day, few statesmen are to be found, who seriously contest the constitutionality of the acts respecting either the embargo, or the purchase and admission of Louisiana into the union.

Why, then, should not that general voice be equally respected in relation to other measures of vast public importance, and by many deemed of still more vital to the country, such as the tariff laws, and the national bank charter?—*Story's Com. v. 3, p. 156. 158. 161, 162.*

Priority of payment of debts, due the United States, out of the estates of debtors who may have died, or become insolvent or bankrupt.

It has been settled upon deliberate argument, that congress possess such a constitutional power. It is a necessary and proper power, to carry into effect the other powers of the government. The government is to pay the debts of the union, and must be authorized to use the means, which appear to itself the most eligible to effect that object.— *Story's Com. v. 3, p. 153.*

43. The object of this clause was to gradually abolish the slave trade, and it is to the honour

The Privilege of the Writ of Habeas Corpus," shall not be suspended, unless when in Cases of Rebellion or Invasion the public Safety may require it.

of America, that she should have set the first example in modern times of abolishing this detestable traffic.

The first clause reported by the convention, allowed each state to perpetuate the slave trade during its pleasure. The question was however finally compromised, by totally abolishing this traffic after the year 1808. The period of twenty years was a necessary sacrifice to the prejudices and interests of a portion of the Southern states.

As soon as the stipulated period of twenty years had expired, congress, by a prospective legislation to meet the exigency, abolished the whole traffic in every direction to citizens and residents. Mild and moderate laws were, however, found insufficient for the purpose of putting an end to the practice; and at length congress found it necessary (See act of Congress 1820, ch. 113,) to declare the slave trade to be a piracy and to punish it with death.—*Story's Com. v.3, p. 204, 205.*

It seems to be the settled opinion that all control over the slaves now in the United States, (District of Columbia excepted) and legislative provision in relation thereto are exclusively vested in the respective states.—*Compiler.*

44. At the common law there are various writs, called writs of habeas corpus. But the particular one here spoken of is that great and celebrated writ, used in all cases of illegal confinement, known by the name of the writ of habeas corpus *ad subjiciendum*, directed to the person arraigning another, and commanding him to produce the body of the

No Bill of Attainder or ex post facto Law shall be passed.[45]

No Capitation, or other direct, Tax shall be laid, unless in Proportion to the Census or

prisoner, with the day and cause of his caption and detention, to do, submit to, and receive, whatsoever the judge or court, awarding such writ, shall consider in that behalf. It is, therefore, justly esteemed the great bulwark of personal liberty; since it is the appropriate remedy to ascertain, whether any person is rightfully in confinement or not, and the cause of his confinement; and if no sufficient ground of detention appears, the party is entitled to his immediate discharge.

It would seem, as the power is given to congress to suspend the writs of habeas corpus in case of rebellion or invasion, that the right to judge whether the exigency had arisen, must exclusively belong to that body.—*Story's Com.* v. 3, *p.* 206. 209.

45. Bills of attainder, as they are technically called, are such special acts of the legislature, as inflict capital punishment upon persons supposed to be guilty of high offences, such as treason and felony, without any conviction in the ordinary course of judicial proceedings.—*Story's Com.* v. 3, *p.* 209.

The terms *ex post facto* laws, in a comprehensive sense, embrace all retrospective laws, or laws governing, or controlling past transactions, whether they are of a civil, or criminal nature.—*Story's Com.* v. 3, *p.* 212.

Laws, however, which *mitigate* the character, or punishment of a crime already committed, may not fall within the prohibition, for they are in favour of the citizen.—*Story's Com.* v. 4, *p.* 213.

Enumeration herein before directed to be taken.[46]

No Tax or Duty shall be laid on articles exported from any State.[47]

No Preference shall be given by any Regulation of Commerce or Revenue to the Ports of one State over those of another:[48] nor shall vessels bound to, or from, one State be obliged to enter, clear, or pay Duties in another.

No Money shall be drawn from the Treasury, but in Consequence of Appropriations made by Law; and a regular Statement and account of the Receipts and Expenditures of all public Money shall be published from time to time.[49]

46. The object of this clause doubtless is, to secure the Southern states against any undue proportion of taxes. The South has a very large slave population; and consequently a pole tax, which should be laid by the rule of uniformity, would operate with peculiar severity on them.—*Story's Com. v. 3, p.* 258.

47. The object of this clause is apparent upon the slightest examination.

48. The obvious object of these provisions is to prevent any possibility of applying the power to lay taxes, or regulate commerce, injuriously to the interest of any one state, so as to favour or aid another.—*Story's Com. v. 2, p.* 469.

49. The object of this clause is to secure regularity, punctuality, and fidelity, in the disbursements of the public money. If it were otherwise, the executive would possess unbounded power over the public purse of the nation; and might apply all its moneyed resources at his pleasure.—*Story's Com. v. 3, p.* 213, 214.

No Title of Nobility shall be granted by the United States;[50] And no Person holding any Office of Profit or Trust under them, shall, without the Consent of the Congress, accept of any present, Emolument, Office, or Title, of any Kind whatever, from any King, Prince, or foreign State.[51]

SECTION 10. No State shall enter into any Treaty, Alliance, or Confederation ;[52] grant Letters of Marque and Reprisal ;[53] coin Money;[54]

50. This clause seems scarcely to require even a passing notice.

51. The other clause, as to acceptance of any emoluments, title, or office, from foreign governments, is founded in a just jealousy of foreign influence of every sort.—*Story's Com. v.* 3, *p.* 216.

52. The prohibition against treaties, alliances, and confederations, constituted a part of the articles of confederation, and was from thence transferred in substance, into the constitution. The sound policy, nay, the necessity of it, for the preservation of any national government, is so obvious, as to strike the most careless mind. If every state were at liberty to enter into any treaties, alliances, or confederacies, with any foreign state, it would become utterly subversive of the power confided to the national government on the same subject.—*Story's Com. v.* 3, *p.* 217, 218.

53. The prohibition to grant letters of marque and reprisal stands upon the same ground.—*Story's Com. v.* 3, *p.* 218.

54. We have already seen, that the power " to coin money, and regulate the value thereof," is

emit Bills of Credit;[55] make any Thing but Gold and Silver Coin a Tender in Payment of Debts; pass any Bill of Attainder, ex post facto Law, or Law impairing the Obligation of Contracts,* or grant any Title of Nobility.

confided to the general government. If the states were permitted to coin money, it would defeat one of the main purposes, for which the power is given to the general government, viz. uniformity of the currency.—*Story's Com. v. 3, p. 220.*

55. What is the true meaning of the phrase "bills of credit" in the constitution? The word "emit" is never employed in describing those contracts, by which a state binds itself to pay money at a future day for services actually received, or for money borrowed for present use. Nor are instruments, executed for such purposes, in common language denominated "bills of credit." To emit bills of credit conveys to the mind the idea of issuing paper, intended to circulate through the

---

* Where a law is in its nature a *contract*, where absolute rights have vested under that contract, a repeal of the law cannot divest those rights. *Fletcher vs. Peck*, 6 *Cranch*, 88.

A party to a contract cannot pronounce its own deed invalid, although that party be a *sovereign state*. *Id.* ib.

A grant is a *contract executed*. *Id.* 89.

A law annulling conveyance is unconstitutional, because it is a law impairing the obligation of contracts within the meaning of the Constitution of the United States. *Id.*

The Court will not declare a law to be unconstitutional, unless the opposition between the Constitution and the law be clear and plain. *Id.* 87.

An act of the Legislature of a State, declaring that certain lands which should be purchased for the Indians should not thereafter be subject to any tax, constituted a contract which could not after the adoption of the Constitution of the United States be rescinded by a subsequent legislative act; such rescinding act being void under the Constitution of the United States. *State of New-Jersey vs. Wilson*, 7 *Cranch*, 164.

community for its ordinary purposes, *as money,* which paper is redeemable at a future day.—*Story's Com. v.* 3, *p.* 227.

The present Constitution of the United States did not commence its operation until the first Wednesday in March, 1789, and the provision in the Constitution that "no State shall make any law impairing the obligation of contracts," does not extend to a State law enacted before that day, and operating upon rights of property vesting before that time. *Owings* vs. *Speed,* 5 *Wheaton,* 420, 421.

An act of a State Legislature which discharges a debtor from all liability for debts contracted previous to his discharge on his surrendering his property for the benefit of his creditors, is a law impairing "the obligations of contracts" within the meaning of the Constitution of the United States, so far as it attempts to discharge the contract; and it makes no difference in such a case, that the suit was brought in a State Court of the state of which both the parties were citizens where the contract was made, and the discharge obtained, and where they continued to reside until the suit was brought. *Farmers' and Mechanics' Bank* vs. *Smith,* 6 *Wheaton,* 131.

The act of New-York, passed on the 3d of April, 1811, (which not only liberates the person of the debtor, but discharges him from all liability for any debts contracted previous to his discharge on his surrendering his property in the manner it prescribes) so far as it attempts to discharge the contract, is a law impairing the obligation of contracts within the meaning of the Constitution of the United States, and is not a good plea in bar of an action brought upon such contract. *Sturges* vs. *Crowningshield,* 4 *Wheaton,* 122. 197.

Statutes of limitation and usury laws, unless retroactive in their effect, do not impair the obligation of contracts, and are constitutional. *Id.* 206.

A State bankrupt, or insolvent law, (which not only liberates the person of the debtor, but discharges him from all liability for the debt,) so far as it attempts to discharge the contract, is repugnant to the Constitution of the United States, and it makes no difference in the application of this principle, whether the law was passed *before* or *after* the debt was contracted. *McMillan* vs. *McNeill,* 4 *Wheaton,* 209.

The charter granted by the British Crown to the trustees of Dartmouth College, in New-Hampshire, in the year 1769, is a contract within the meaning of that clause of the Constitution of the United States, (art. 1, sec. 10.) which declares, that no State shall make any law impairing the obligations of contracts. The charter was not dissolved by the Revolution. *College* vs. *Woodard,* 4 *Wheaton,* 518.

An act of the State Legislature of New-Hampshire, altering the charter of Dartmouth College in a material respect, without the consent of the corporation, is an act impairing the obligation of the charter, and is unconstitutional and void. *Id.* 518.

In the convention that framed the constitution the term "bills of credit" was well known and generally understood to indicate the paper currency, issued by the states, during their colonial dependence. During the war of our revolution, the paper currency issued by congress was constantly denominated in the acts of that body, "bills of credit," and the like appellation was applied.—*Story's Com. v. 3, p. 227, 228.*

"Make nothing but Gold or Silver coin a tender," &c.

This clause was manifestly founded on the same general policy, which procured the adoption of the preceding clause, viz. uniformity of currency. *Story's Com. v. 3, p. 236.*

"Pass any bill of attainder, or ex post facto law, or law impairing the obligation of contract."

The two former require no commentary, beyond what has been already offered, under a similar prohibitory clause applied to the government of the United States. The same policy and principles apply to each. (See page .)—*Story's Com. v. 3, p. 238.*

"Law impairing the obligation of a contract."

The Federalist very justly observes that bills of attainder, ex post facto laws, and laws impairing the obligation of contracts are contrary to the just principles of the social compact, and to every principle of sound legislation.

The same author, at the time the adoption of the federal constitution was under consideration, further observed "That, the sober people of America have seen with regret and indignation, that sudden changes and legislative interferences in cases affecting personal rights became jobs in the hands of enterprising and influential speculators, and snares to the more industrious and less informed part of the community."

In order to a just conception of the term impair the obligation of contract it is proper that we consider

1st. What is a contract?
2d. What is the obligation of a contract?
3d. What is impairing a contract?
4th. To what classes of laws does the prohibition apply?
5th. To what extent does it reach, so as to control prospective legislation?

Answer.

1st. A contract is a compact entered into between two persons, to do or not do a particular thing. A contract is executory, or executed. An executory contract is one, in which a party binds himself to do, or not to do a particular thing. An executed contract is one, in which the object of the contract is performed. This differs in nothing from a grant.

Every grant (whether by the legislature or otherwise) in its own nature amounts to an extinguishment of the right of the grantor, and implies a contract not to reassert it.

Contracts too, are express or implied. *Express* contracts are where the terms of the agreement are openly avowed, and uttered at the time of the making it. *Implied* contracts are such, as reason and justice dictate from the nature of the transaction, and which therefore the law presumes, every man undertakes to perform.

The larger class of contracts in civil society, in the ordinary transactions of life are implied. (Example. If at the request of a person I were to do a piece of work for him, without any stipulated price, it would be an implied contract, and the law would allow me a fair and reasonable compensation for my services.)—*Compiler.*

2d. What is the obligation of a contract?

Ans. Whatever I, by my contract, give another a right to require of me. I, by that act, lay myself under an obligation to yield or bestow. It is generally understood that the existing laws of the state in which the contract is made if made by citizens of the state, such for instance as relate to insolvency, limitation of payment, and the like are taken into consideration and constitute a part of the contract, and that no law passed subsequent to the making of the contract, can affect the claims or liabilities of the parties, existing by law at the time of making the contract.

3d. What may properly be deemed impairing the obligation of contracts in the sense of the constitution?

It is perfectly clear, that any law, which enlarges, abridges, or in any manner changes the *intention of the parties*, resulting from the stipulations on the contract, necessarily impairs it.

No one however will doubt, that the legislature may vary the nature and extent of remedies, so that always some substantive remedy be left.

A state legislature may discharge a party from imprisonment upon a judgment in a civil case of contract without infringing the constitution; for this is but a modification of the remedy, and does not impair the obligation of the contract.

The question as to the constitutionality of state insolvent laws was for a long time elaborately discussed. The question is now however understood to be finally at rest; the Supreme Court having decided that state laws in relation to insolvency, existing at the time of making a contract, are taken into consideration by the parties, and are to be considered as constituting a part of the contract.

Still a very important point remains to be examined; and that is, to what contracts such laws

No State shall, without the Consent of the Congress, lay any Imposts or Duties on Imports or Exports, except what may be absolutely necessary for executing its inspection Laws: and the net Produce of all Duties and Imposts, laid by any State on Imports or Exports, shall be for the Use of the Treasury of the United States; and all such Laws shall be subject to the Revision and Controul of the Congress.[56]

can rightfully apply. The result of the various decisions is: 1st. That they apply to all contracts made within the state between citizens of the state; 2d. That they do not apply to contracts made within the state between a citizen of a state, and a citizen of another state; 3d. That they do not apply to contracts not made within the state. And it may be added that, state insolvent laws have no operation whatsoever on contracts made with the United States; for such contracts are, in no manner whatsoever, subject to state jurisdiction. The Supreme Court have also decided that no law passed subsequent to the making of a contract, can annul the claims and the liabilities of the parties, existing at the time of the making of the contract.—*Substance of Story's Com. v. 3, p.* 240 *to* 265.

56. By this article, sufficient provision is made for the convenient arrangement of the domestic and internal trade of the states, whenever it is not injurious to the public interest.

State inspection laws are not, strictly speaking, regulations of commerce, though they may have a remote and considerable influence on commerce. The object of inspection laws, is, to improve the quality of the articles produced by the labour of a country; to fit them for exportation, or for domestic

No State shall, without the Consent of Congress, lay any Duty of tonnage, keep Troops, or Ships of War in time of Peace, enter into any Agreement or Compact with another State, or with a foreign Power, or engage in War, unless actually invaded, or in such imminent Danger as will not admit of delay.[57]

use. Inspection laws, quarantine laws, and health laws, as well as laws for regulating the internal commerce of a state, &c. are component parts of state legislation, resulting from the residuary powers of state sovereignty.—*Story's Com. v. 2, p. 473.*

57. The first part of this clause, respecting laying a duty on tonnage, has been already considered. The remaining clauses have their origin in the same general policy and reasoning, which forbid any state from entering into any treaty, alliance, or confederation; and from granting letters of marque and reprisal.

In regard to treaties, alliances, and confederation; they are wholly prohibited. But a state may, *with the consent of congress*, enter into an agreement, or compact, with another state, or with a foreign power. The terms "compact and agreement," here made use of apply to such only as regards what may be deemed mere private rights of sovereignty; such as questions of boundary; interest in lands, situate in the territories of each other, and other internal regulations for the mutual comfort and convenience of the states bordering on each other. The other prohibitions in the clause respect the power of declaring war which is appropriately confided to the national government.

A state however may be so situated, that it may become indispensable to possess military forces to

ARTICLE II.

SECTION 1. The Executive Power shall be vested in a President of the United States of America. He shall hold his office during the Term of four Years,* and, together with the Vice-President, chosen for the same Term, be elected, as follows:

Each State shall appoint, in such Manner as the Legislature thereof may direct,†⁵⁸ a Number

resist an expected invasion or insurrection. The danger may be too imminent for delay; and under such circumstances, a state will have a right to raise troops for its own safety, even without the consent of congress.—*Story's Com. v. 3, p. 273.*

58. Some states choose their electors by the legislature, some by districts, and others by general ticket.

No question has ever arisen, as to the constitutionality of either mode, except that of a direct choice by the legislature. The constitutionality of this method has been doubted by some able and ingenuous minds, but as the practice has been sanctioned ever since the adoption of the constitution, the question does not seem to admit of controversy: there is moreover no existing tribunal to adjudicate upon it.

For the sake of uniformity, it has been thought desirable by some statesmen, that the constitution should be so amended as to provide for a uniform mode of choice by the people.

In the original plan, as well as in the amendment,

---

* See Laws of the U. States, vol. ii, ch. 109, sec. 12.
† See Laws of the U. States, vol. ii, ch. 109.

of Electors, equal to the whole Number of Senators and Representatives to which the State may be entitled in the Congress: but no Senator or Representative, or Person holding an Office of Trust or Profit under the United States, shall be appointed an Elector.[59]

no provision is made for the discussion or decision of any questions, which may arise, as to the regularity or authenticity of the returns of the electoral votes, or the rights of the persons, who gave the votes, or the manner, or circumstances, in which they ought to be counted. It seems to have been taken for granted, that no question could ever arise on the subject; and that nothing more was necessary than to open the certificates, which were produced, in presence of both houses, and to count the names and numbers as returned. Another defect in the constitution is, that no provision was originally, or is now made, for a case, where there is an equality of votes by the electors for more persons than the constitutional number, from which the house of representatives is to make the election. Suppose there should be four candidates; two of whom should have an equality of votes; who are to be preferred? Such a case is quite within the range of probability; and may hereafter occasion very serious dissensions.—*Story's Com. v. 3, p. 327, 328, 329.*

59. The object of the clause precluding any senator, public officer, &c. from being an elector, is, to prevent persons holding a public station under the United States government, from exercising any direct influence in the choice of President.—*Story's Com. v. 3, p. 327, 328, 329.*

* The Electors shall meet in their respective States, and vote by Ballot for two Persons, of whom one at least shall not be an Inhabitant of the same state with themselves. And they shall make a List of all the Persons voted for, and of the number of votes for each; which List they shall sign and certify, and transmit sealed to the Seat of the Government of the United States, directed to the President of the Senate. The President of the Senate shall, in the Presence of the Senate and House of Representatives, open all the Certificates, and the Votes shall then be counted. The Person having the greatest Number of votes shall be the President, if such Number be a Majority of the whole Number of Electors appointed; and if there be more than one who have such Majority, and have an equal Number of votes, then the House of Representatives shall immediately chuse by Ballot one of them for President; and if no Person have a Majority, then from the five highest on the List the said House shall in like manner chuse the President. But in chusing the President, the Votes shall be taken by States, the Representation from each State having one Vote; a quorum for this Purpose shall consist of a Member or Members from two thirds of the States, and a Majority of all the States shall be necessary to a Choice. In every Case, after the Choice of the President, the Person having the greatest Number of Votes of the Electors shall be the Vice

---

* Vide Amendments, art. 12.

President. But if there should remain two or more who have equal Votes, the Senate shall chuse from them by Ballot the Vice President.*

The Congress may determine the Time of chusing the Electors,† and the Day on which they shall give their Votes; which Day shall be the same throughout the United States.‡[60]

[Considering that the comments in relation to the choice of president and vice-president, have reference principally to the twelfth amendment to the constitution, the compiler has thought proper to insert the same in this place.]

ARTICLE THE TWELFTH. The Electors shall meet in their respective States, and vote by ballot for President and Vice President, one of whom, at least, shall not be an inhabitant of the same State with themselves; they shall name in their ballots the person voted for as President, and in distinct ballots the person voted for as Vice President, and they shall make distinct

---

60. The propriety of this power would seem to be almost self-evident. Such a measure is calculated to repress political intrigues and speculations, by rendering a combination among the electoral colleges, as to their votes, if not utterly impracticable, at least very difficult.—*Story's Com.* v. 3, p. 330.

---

* This clause is annulled. See Amendments, art. 12.
† See Laws of the U. States, vol. ii, ch. 104, sec. 1.
‡ See Laws of the U. States, vol. ii, ch. 109, sec. 2.

lists of all Persons voted for as President, and of all Persons voted for as Vice-President, and of the number of votes for each, which lists they shall sign and certify, and transmit sealed to the seat of the Government of the United States, directed to the President of the Senate :—The President of the Senate shall, in the presence of the Senate and House of Representatives, open all the Certificates and the votes shall then be counted;—The person having the greatest number of votes for President, shall be the President, if such number be a majority of the whole number of Electors appointed; and if no person have such majority, then from the persons having the highest numbers not exceeding three on the list of those voted for as President, the house of Representatives shall choose immediately, by ballot, the President. But in choosing the President, the votes shall be taken by States, the representation from each State having one vote; a quorum for this purpose shall consist of a Member or Members from two-thirds of the States, and a majority of all the States shall be necessary to a choice. And if the house of Representatives shall not choose a President whenever the right of choice shall devolve upon them, before the fourth day of March next following, then the Vice President shall act as President, as in the case of the death or other Constitutional disability of the President. The Person having the greatest number of votes as Vice President, shall be the Vice President, if such number be a majority of the whole number of Electors appointed, and if no person have a Majority, then from the two highest numbers on the list, the Senate shall choose the Vice President; a quorum for the purpose shall consist of two-thirds of the whole number of Senators, and a majority of the whole number shall be necessary to a choice. But no person constitutionally ineligible to the office of President shall be eligible to that of Vice President of the United States.

No Person except a natural born Citizen, or a Citizen of the United States, at the time of the adoption of this Constitution, shall be eligible to the Office of President; neither shall any Person be eligible to that Office who shall not have attained to the Age of thirty-five Years, and been fourteen years a Resident within the United States.[61]

In Case of the Removal of the President from office, or of his Death, Resignation,* or inability

---

61. It is a great fundamental policy of all governments to exclude foreign influence from their executive councils and duties.

By "residence" in the constitution, is to be understood, not an absolute inhabitancy within the United States, during the whole period; but such an inhabitancy, as includes a permanent domicil in the United States. No one has supposed, that a temporary residence abroad, on public business, and especially on an embassy to a foreign nation, would interrupt the residence of a citizen, so as to disqualify him for office.—*Story's Com. v. 3, p. 333.*

---

* See Laws of the U. States, vol. ii, ch. 104, sec. 11

to discharge the Powers and Duties of said Office, the same shall devolve on the Vice-President, and the Congress may by Law provide for the Case of Removal, Death, Resignation or Inability, both of the President and Vice-President, declaring what officer shall then act as President,[63] and such Officer shall act accordingly, until the Disability be removed, or a President shall be elected.*

62. Congress, in pursuance of the power here given, have provided, that in case of the removal, death, resignation, or inability of the president and vice president, the president of the senate pro tempore, and in case there shall be no president, pro tempore, then the speaker of the house of representatives for the time being shall act as president, until the disability be removed, or a president shall be elected.†

If the office should devolve on the speaker, after the congress, for which the last speaker was chosen, had expired, and before the next meeting of congress, it might be a question, who is to serve? and whether the speaker of the house of representatives, then extinct, could be deemed the person intended. In order to provide for the exigency of a vacancy in the office of president during the recess of congress, it has become usual for the vice president, a few days before the termination of each session of congress, to retire from the chair of the senate, to enable that body to elect a president, pro tempore, to be ready to act in any case of emergency.— *Story's Com. v. 3, p.* 335.

---

* See Laws of the U. States, vol. ii, ch. 109, sec. 9; and vol. iii, ch. 403.
† Act of 1st March, 1792, ch. 8.

The President shall, at stated Times, receive for his Services, a Compensation, which shall neither be increased nor diminished during the Period for which he shall have been elected, and he shall not receive within that Period any Emolument from the United States, or any of them.

Before he enter on the Execution of his Office, he shall take the following oath or Affirmation :—"I do solemnly swear (or affirm) that I will faithfully execute the Office of President of the United States, and will to the best of my Ability, preserve, protect and defend the Constitution of the United States."

SECTION 2. The President shall be Commander in Chief of the Army and Navy of the United States, and of the Militia of the several States, when called into the actual Service of the United States;* he may require the Opinion, in writing, of the principal Officer in each of the executive Departments, upon any Subject relating to the Duties of their respective Offices, and he shall have power to grant Reprieves and

---

* The act of the State of Pennsylvania, of the 28th of March, 1814, (providing, sec. 21, that the officers and privates of the Militia of that State neglecting or refusing to serve when called into actual service, in pursuance of any order or requisition of the President of the U. States, shall be liable to the penalties defined in the act of Congress, of 28th February, 1795, ch. 277, or to any penalty which may have been prescribed since the date of that act, or which may hereafter be prescribed by any law of the United States, and also providing for the trial of such delinquents by a State Court Martial, and that a list of the delinquents fined by such court should be furnished to the Marshal of the U. States, &c.; and also to the Comptroller of the Treasury of the United States, in order that the further proceedings directed to be had thereon by the laws of the United States might be completed,) is not repugnant to the Constitution and Laws of the United States.—*Houston* vs. *Moore*, 5 *Wheaton*, 1. 12.

Pardons for offences against the United States, except in Cases of Impeachment.[63]

63. The most that ever has been, and ever can be done, is to provide for the punishment of crimes by some general rules, and within some general limitations. The total exclusion of all power of pardon would necessarily introduce a very dangerous power in judges and juries, of following the spirit, rather than the letter of the laws; or, out of humanity, of suffering real offenders wholly to escape punishment.

A power therefore to pardon seems, indeed, indispensable under the most correct administration of the law by human tribunals; since, otherwise, men would sometimes fall a prey to the vindictiveness of accusers, the inaccuracy of testimony, and the fallability of jurors and courts. If an arbitrary power is to be given to meet such cases, where can it be so properly lodged, as in the executive department?—*Story's Com. v.* 3, *p.* 345.

There is an exception to the power of pardon, that it shall not extend to cases of impeachment. As judgment for an offence of this kind extends no farther than a removal from office, and disqualification to hold office, there are not the same reasons and necessity for the exercise of the pardoning power as in cases where the life or liberty of a citizen is involved.—*Story's Com. v.* 3, *p.* 352.

It is further worthy of consideration, that persons holding high official stations are nominated by the president, and by a fixed construction of the constitution, are liable to be removed at his pleasure. Thus situated, a person in a lucrative situation might be induced to prostitute the purposes of his office, in order to promote the ambitious views of the executive. For these and other reasons, the

He shall have Power, by and with the Advice
and Consent of the Senate, to make Treaties,[64]
provided two-thirds of the Senators present
concur; and he shall nominate, and by and
with the Advice and Consent of the Senate,
shall appoint Ambassadors, other public Ministers and Consuls, Judges of the Supreme Court,
and all other Officers of the United States,
whose Appointments are not herein otherwise
provided for, and which shall be established by
Law:[65] but the Congress may by Law vest the

constitution has wisely interposed this check upon
his power, so that he cannot, by any corrupt coalition with favourites, or dependants in high offices,
screen them from punishment.—*Story's Com. v. 3,
p.* 352.

Treaties.

64. The power to make treaties is, by the constitution, general; and of course it embraces all sorts
of treaties, for peace or war; for commerce or territory; for alliance or succours, &c.

But though the power is thus general and unrestricted, it is not to be so construed, as to destroy
the fundamental laws of the state. A power given
by the constitution cannot be so construed as to
authorize a destruction of other powers in the
same instrument.—*Story's Com. v.* 3, *p.* 355.

Although the president may ask the advice and
consent of the senate to a treaty, he is not absolutely bound by it; for he may after it is given,
still constitutionally refuse to ratify it.—*Story's Com.
v.* 3, *p.* 371, 372.

65. The power *to nominate* does not naturally or
necessarily, include the power *to remove;* and if the
power to *appoint* does include it, then the latter belongs conjointly to the executive and the senate.

Appointment of such inferior Officers, as they think proper, in the President alone, in the Courts of Law, or in the Heads of Departments.

This was the doctrine maintained with great earnestness by the author of the Federalist, one of the most distinguished framers of the constitution, whose writings in favour of that instrument appeared about the time of its adoption by the states. (See Federalist, No. 77.) Its language is, "*The consent of that body* (the senate) *would be necessary to displace as well as to appoint.*" This view of the subject had a most material tendency to quiet the just alarms of the people as to the overwhelming influence, and arbitrary exercise of this prerogative by the executive, which might prove fatal to the *personal independence, and freedom of opinion of public officers, as well as to the public liberties of the country.*

In the first draft of the constitution, the exclusive power was given to the president to appoint officers in all cases not otherwise provided for by the constitution, and the advice and consent of the senate was not required. But in the same draft, the power to appoint ambassadors and judges of the Supreme Court was given to the senate. The advice and consent of the senate, and the appointment by the president of ambassadors, and ministers, consuls, and judges of Supreme Court, was afterwards reported by a committee, as an amendment, and was unanimously adopted.

In answer to the remarks of a member of the convention, who was in favour of giving the president the exclusive appointment of some officers, Mr. Roger Sherman observed, "That he esteemed the provision made for appointments to be a matter of great importance—one on which the liberties and safety of the people depended nearly as much as on legislation. If the appointing power, continued Mr. S., was vested in the president alone, he might render himself despotic. It was the saying of one of the kings of England, *that 'while the king could appoint the bishops and judges, he might have what religion and laws he pleased.'* To give that observation its full effect, they must hold their offices during his pleasure. By such appointments, without control, a power might be gradually established, that would be more formidable than a standing army."

During the first congress, a bill was reported, establishing the department of foreign affairs. In framing this law, it became an important subject of inquiry, in what manner, or by whom, this important officer could be removed from office. This was a question as new, as it was important, and was applicable to all other offices of executive appointment. Before that period, no power of removal other than by the president and senate had been avowed by the friends of the constitution, although it was urged by its opponents, as a reason for rejecting it. The principal question on which congress were divided, was, whether they were removable by the president alone, or by the president in concurrence with the senate. A majority, however, in both houses decided, that this power was in the president alone. In the house, the majority in favour of this construction was twelve; the senate were equally divided, and the casting vote was given by the vice president. In opposition to the power of removal by the president, it was urged in the first place—"That it was improper for the legislature, in this manner, to give a construction to the constitution;—in the second place, it was said that this great and important power, by a fair construction of the constitution, was in the president and senate. It was further said, that the constitution being silent on the question, it was contrary to sound policy, as well as inconsistent with the principles of a free government, to give by construction, such power to any one individual—that it was liable to great abuses, and would render officers entirely dependant on the will, perhaps the whim and caprice of one man.

In answer to these objections, and in favour of giving the president the power of removal, it was said, that facts in relation to the *malconduct* of an officer, might come to the knowledge of the president, rendering an immediate removal indispensable; and the delay of convening the senate, might be fatal to the best interests of the community. With respect to removals, from whim, caprice, or unworthy motives, it was alleged, that sufficient checks were provided against such a wanton abuse of power. It was also stated by some members, particularly by Mr. Lawrence and Mr. Madison, that for such a wanton abuse of power, the president himself would be liable to impeachment and removal from office.

The danger then, Mr. Madison observed, consists in this, the president can displace from office, a man whose merits require that he should continue in it. In the first place, (continued Mr. M.,) he will be impeachable by this house, before the senate, for such an act of maladministration; for I contend, that the wanton removal of meritorious officers, would subject him to impeachment, and removal from his own high trust.*

---

* Pitkin's Hist. United States, vol. ii, p. 328, 329. Marshall's Life of Washington, vol. v, p. 196–200. Story's Com. vol. iii, p. 371. 384. 390. 392.

During the administration of Washington, no removals were made without cause; few or none in that of the first President Adams, a considerable increase in numbers during Mr. Jefferson's administration, but with an express disclaimer of the right to remove for differences of opinion, or otherwise than for some clear public good. In the administrations of the subsequent Presidents, Madison, Monroe, and John Q. Adams, a general moderation and forbearance were exercised, and no instances of removal, as is believed took place, except such as were warranted by the construction given by the first congress to the constitution.

Since the induction into office of President Jackson, it seems that all the evils, anticipated by those members of the first congress who were opposed to the construction given to the constitution by that body, have been fully realized; but that the remedy pointed out by Mr. Lawrence, Mr. Madison, and others, has not been applied. A wonderful, if not an alarming extension of the removing and appointing power, under the administration of President Jackson, compared with that of his predecessors, has taken place, as will appear from the following statement, which has been repeatedly published, and never, as is believed denied.

Removals.

During the 8 years of Washington's administration, there were...					11
"	4	"	John Adams	"	11
"	8	"	Thomas Jefferson	"	39
"	8	"	James Madison	"	5
"	8	"	James Monroe	"	9
"	4	"	John Quincy Adams*	"	2
Total number of removals, during 40 years....					77

* A gentleman of undoubted veracity informed the compiler of this work, that certain friends of Mr. Adams, during

Being about two each year. And considering the number of offices held in the United States, it must be admitted that the small number of removals, indicates as a whole, great fidelity on the part of the officers, a judicious selection by the executives, and a just, generous, and liberal spirit on the part of those intrusted with the appointing power.

	Removals.	
During the first year and twenty days of President Jackson's administration, there were removed, including heads of departments, foreign ministers, consuls, collectors of customs, naval officers, surveyors of ports, and other officers..............	231	
Postmasters, as appears by the Postmaster General's Report of 24th March, 1830................	491	
		722
Subordinate officers of customs...................	151	
Deputy collectors, clerks in customs, deputy marshals, private secretaries to foreign ministers, clerks in the land and other offices, &c..........	600	
		751
		1473

The forty years' silence and general acquiescence of the people, particularly the rigid constructionists in the construction given to the constitution, as re-

---

some period of his presidency, advised him that a number of persons, holding lucrative stations under the general government, were opposing his re-election—and recommended him to remove them from office—to which Mr. A. replied that neither the constitution nor laws authorized him to interfere with the political views or partialities of any one—that he had the right to remove only such as were unfaithful to the trust reposed in them by *law*—and that he should not assume the right for any other cause. If, continued Mr. A., it were reduced to a certainty, that the removal of one of the lowest officers, except for such reasons as I have mentioned, would secure my re-election, I would not do it—I would rather lose the support, said he, of the people by such a course of conduct, than to gain it through an indirect bribe, and by trampling upon the constitution.—*Compiler.*

spects the appointing power, can be accounted for in no other manner, as is believed, than from the fact, that during that period, the power was only exercised with strict reference to the public good, and to the faithful execution of the laws.

For several years past, a strong effort has been made in several states, particularly in New-York, by leading politicians, to vest the appointing power in the hands of a few, and to give offices to none but those of a particular party. In the convention of the state of New-York that framed a new constitution during the year 1821, there were two prominent parties upon the question relating to the appointing power—one was in favour of giving the choice of sheriffs and clerks of counties, coroners, and other officers, usually receiving liberal emoluments *directly to the people.*—The other was in favour of having them appointed by the Governor alone, the Governor and Senate, or in some manner other than *that of a direct choice by the people.* And it is a singular fact, that many who advocated the latter method, have for years, owing as is believed to inducements held out by the appointing power, been in the successful tide of political advancement, and of popular favour. The same proscriptive policy and party favouritism, which for years have lessened the political character of the state of New-York, have it seems been introduced at Washington, and it will be readily perceived, that the exclusive control, by one man, of the vast amount of patronage, afforded by the general government, cannot fail of giving him a most potent influence, and a control over the actions of his fellow-citizens more formidable than guns and bayonets. It also tends to create a servile dependence, and to otherwise debase and degrade the human character; and should the practice of dispensing the government patronage to none but political favourites continue, there is reason to fear, that under the blind party rage which such a course is calculated to produce, the best interests of the country will be neglected or kept out of view,—that one faction will successively rise up to immolate another—that violence will succeed violence—until some ambitious chieftain, viewing the political degradation of one party, and the disgust and indifference of the other, will, at a single blow, annihilate the form and existence of our republican institutions. This, to some, may appear too dark a picture, even for the imagination. The compiler has only to say, that he hopes, that in any event, time will show his fears to have been unfounded, and that none of the anticipated evils arising from the appointing power have been realized. He would rather suffer all the disgrace attached to a false prophet, than one jot or tittle of his apprehensions should be fulfilled.

Having pointed out, what the compiler conceives to be a cardinal defect either in the constitution itself, or in the construction given to that instrument, it is proper for him to say, that he has ever considered it due from a person, pointing out what he may consider to be any material error, either in the laws or constitution of his country, to suggest, at the same time, some modification, or an entire substitute. Acting upon the principle recommended to others, the compiler respectfully proceeds, but with great diffidence, to offer his views upon a proposed amendment to the constitution.

The compiler's diffidence is doubly enhanced, from the fact that, in the first place, but few persons to whom he ever suggested his scheme, has fully approved of it, from a conviction, as was alleged, of its impracticability; and, in the second place, that the compiler is opposed to any alteration in, or innovation upon the constitution, excepting in such parts as experience shall have clearly and fully proved are productive of bad consequences, or where its general object and intention are not effected. The compiler is, moreover, of opinion, that it would be better to suffer some inconveniences and bad consequences, than to run the risk of any alterations or amendments, excepting such as experience, calm reflection, and sound judgment would justify.

With these preliminary remarks, the compiler would observe that he has long been satisfied, from deep reflection, that the *appointing power* ought to be as separate and distinct from the legislative and executive, as that of the *judiciary*,—and that an appointing power should be created, wholly unconnected with legislative or other government duties; giving the executive the right of removing any officer, for neglect of duty or other improper conduct.

By this plan, the duties of the legislative and executive power would be confined to such questions of national policy as immediately concern the happiness and welfare of the people. Deprived of an opportunity of bestowing, directly or indirectly, any government patronage upon any one, members of congress and the executive could expect no favour or support on that account; and, indeed, the only support and good opinion they could expect to receive from their fellow-citizens would be from the wisdom of their measures. As artful and ambitious office seekers could expect to receive no particular aid from the executive or legislative department, in the furtherance of their views, no unjust or unreasonable opposition to their labours, need to be feared from such a source. The great majority of the people are honest, and feel their happiness and welfare to be identified with good government; and when left free to exercise their sober and honest opinion, uninfluenced by artful and ambitious demagogues, they will generally form a correct opinion.

It is true that some management, as it is called, would naturally exist in devising ways and means to secure a seat in congress; but as no government patronage could be given or even promised, the motives to favour the views and wishes of an improper person would be greatly diminished from what it is under the present order of things.

It may perhaps be urged, in the first place, that the President not having the appointment of officers, the laws would not be so faithfully executed as though he appointed them himself. And, in the second place, that cases might arise in which the public good might require the removal of an officer without any specific charges:—and, third, that the President might, from unjustifiable motives, remove meritorious officers.

In answer to the first objection—the officer would feel equally as responsible as though he received his appointment from the President.

Secondly. It is believed that the duties and liabilities of public officers can be so precisely defined by law, as, on the one hand, to warrant the performance of their duties with faithfulness and satisfaction to the public; and, on the other hand, to embrace all such exigencies as would warrant their removal.

In considering what *might be done*, it is proper also to take into view probabilities. The President, from the proposed plan is so situated, that, in ordinary cases, he could have no motive, other than the public good, in removing a meritorious officer, as the appointing of a successor would devolve upon the appointing power.

Without, however, theorizing further upon this subject, the constitution of the state of New-York may be cited as a case analogous to the plan here proposed. In that state, sheriffs, county clerks, &c., are, by its constitution, elected by the people;—the governor possessing the right of removal for improper conduct. These, as must be admitted, are state, as well as county officers. The plan has been in operation twelve years,—and only two removals, it is believed, have, during that time, been made by the Governor, and those received the unanimous support of all political parties. The people are satisfied with the plan—the sheriffs and clerks are generally of different politics in different counties; but seldom, if ever, are complaints made as to the discharge of their official duties: and, so far as the observation of the compiler has extended, and from the best of information, he feels himself warranted in saying, that better and more faithful officers are chosen by the people, than when appointed by the council of appointment, consisting of the Governor and four senators.

It may be urged, that intrigue and management will be resorted to, in order to influence the appointing power. In answer to this, it may be said, that it would depend in a great measure upon the manner in which that body is constituted; but it is believed, that, from the experience of forty-five years, which we have already had, the sources of corruption are generally known, and that all its usual avenues may be so guarded, as to insure the public a judicious selection of officers: but, even admitting a bad selection should occasionally be made, there is still a check vested in the President, who, from the manner in which he is placed, we have reason to suppose, would exercise his high trust with as much impartiality as a Chancellor or Judge of the Supreme Court. We, moreover, could confidently calculate that the selection of public officers would be as good, as under the present system. The community, therefore, by adopting the proposed plan, would at farthest lose nothing upon the score of the appointment of public officers, but would *gain* a legislative and executive department, uninfluenced by any consideration, other than the public good.

Whilst upon the subject of the appointing power, the compiler thinks he may to advantage, offer a few remarks upon a subject, which, although totally disconnected with the question of the appointing power, is a theme of considerable animadversion by some, and apparently alarm by others. The subject alluded to is the BANKING SYSTEM. It is contended by some, that the present banking system, and particularly the Bank of the United States, is more dangerous to the liberties of this country than the appointing power.

A few facts and illustrations will show the fallacy of this kind of reasoning.

The President of the United States has, in effect, the principal control of the whole government patronage. The Senate, it is admitted, may occasionally resist an odious nomination; but, after all, the President, having the right of nomination, can compel that body to either confirm the nomination of one of his partisans, or incur the odium of stopping the operations of government. This patronage must necessarily be confined to a favoured few; as for example, as the law now is, there can be but one collector, one postmaster, one surveyor, &c., for New-York, or any other city. Now, if there were but one bank in the United States, and if that bank were so constituted, as in effect to give the control of its favours to one man, or at most a select few, and if they were restrained by law, in dispensing any favours to any but a certain number provided by law, say like the collector, postmaster, surveyor, &c., with their subordinate officers; then, indeed, might there be just grounds of fear, as to the stability of our republican institutions—the bank could, undoubtedly, control the government, and the whole country. It would in reality be more formidable to the liberties of the people than a standing army.

But the very reverse of this is the case. There are, in the United States more than six hundred banks, and the loaning of money is in reality as much a species of trade, as that of selling molasses, tea, or any other kind of merchandise. Whenever a merchant is about giving credit to a person, he does not stop to inquire whether his proposed customer is a supporter of General Jackson or Mr. Clay; but his first first inquiry will be, whether he is a man of responsibility, and whether his (the merchant's) interest will be promoted in giving a credit ; and if so, the credit will be given. The purchaser on his part, will take into view the price of the merchant's goods, and the length of credit offered. If both are satisfied, a bargain will be consummated. This is what may be termed mutual dependence; and wherever it pervades human society, it is impossible, from the very nature of the principle, that any thing like oppression or servility can exist. The same rules of dependence or control that govern fair and honourable mercantile transactions, will apply in its fullest extent to the banking system; and the compiler does not hesitate to say, that the banking system as now constituted, and with its present competition, is no more dangerous to the liberties of this country than agriculture, commerce, and manufactures.

Nor can the compiler see how the United States Bank, saying nothing of its great national benefits, can exercise an influence any more dangerous to the liberties of the country than the state banks. The capital, it is admitted, is large; but it must be borne in mind, that this capital is distributed among twenty states, so that the capital of several of the branches is less than that of some of the state banks; but, suppose that were not the case, the position must be first established, in order to prove the danger arising from the United States Bank on account of its large capital,—that an institution of this kind, with a capital of one hundred thousand dollars, is less dangerous to civil liberty than one with a capital of one million of dollars; or, in other words, that the danger to civil liberty increases in exact ratio with the increase of capital. A position which, it is believed, no conscientious or well informed man would attempt to sustain.*

---

* A bank, it will be admitted, *might, or perhaps could*, with its money, if not loaned out, hire thieves and assassins to commit the most flagrant felonies; and if they should happen to be indicted, they *might* bribe a court and jury to acquit them; they also *might, and perhaps could*, employ their agents to buy up votes for a particular candidate, at an election; or to commit other crimes and misdemeanours.

So might, and so could, the canal commissioners break down, at some place, the embankment of the Erie Canal, and not only deluge the whole adjacent country, but stop the transportation by water, of the whole produce of the west, and thus deprive the state of its canal tolls. The engineer of a steamboat might, by a very simple process, blow the boat and its passengers to atoms; and a man intrusted with a razor, *might and could* cut his own throat. These are all within the range of *possibilities*, but of very remote *probabilities*. The reader, at first view, may consider this to be an extraordinary simile; but, considering the manner in which banks are constituted, a little reflection, it is believed, will satisfy any one that it is neither extravagant nor unreasonable. The capital of a bank is made up of stock—the stock is usually divided into shares of from twenty-five to one hundred dollars—these shares are owned by individuals of different religions, and of different politics, and are transferable; hundreds of shares, particularly in large cities, being daily bought and sold like any kind of merchandise.— Par value is the original cost of the stock at the time of sub-

There will, undoubtedly, be seasons of scarcity
of money; or, in other words, when the demand

---

scribing—if stock, which, at the time of subscribing, cost
$100, be sold for $110, it is said to be ten per cent. *above* par
—if it be sold for $95, it is said to be five per cent. *below* par.
The price of stock is regulated by various circumstances—
the concerns of a bank are generally managed by a board of
from thirteen to twenty-five directors, chosen by the stockholders—foreigners own a considerable amount of stock in
the banks of this country; and in several of the state banks
have a right to vote, on their stock for directors; but no
foreigner, owning stock in the Bank of the United States, can
vote for directors of that institution—he puts his money completely under the control of citizens of the United States—
the president and cashier of a bank are generally chosen by
its directors—the object of banking institutions is to loan
money, and make as great a dividend to the stockholders as
they lawfully can—the interest on loans made by the United
States Bank is limited by law to six per cent.—banks in
the state of New-York, under the safety fund law, have a
right to charge seven per cent. on loans exceeding sixty
days. The foregoing are the principal and leading features
in the construction and operation of a bank; and we confidently appeal to the candour of any one to say, whether he
believes there is any greater probability of the directors applying its funds for unlawful purposes, than of the canal
commissioners wilfully doing such an act, in relation to the
Erie Canal, as would not only destroy its public benefit, but at
the same time sacrifice the pecuniary interests of the state.
Let the reader suppose himself to be the owner of stock in a
bank, and then consider whether he could be induced to vote
for directors that were in the habit of squandering its funds at
the polls of popular elections, or for any purpose other than
the legitimate one contemplated in the bank charter. The
history of the bank operations of this country, it is admitted,
shows some instances in which directors, presidents, cashiers,
or clerks, have proved faithless to the trust reposed in them,
by applying the funds of a bank to their individual use and
benefit: the amount, however, thus squandered has, of late
years been small, bearing but a little proportion to the capital
vested; and wherever frauds of this kind have been committed, they have not affected the civil liberties of the country, but in all cases, the stockholders of the bank; and in
some cases, the holders of the bills: and it is reasonable to

will be greater than the supply: the same contingency will happen with respect to flour, and various

---

conclude, that on a question so deeply affecting the interests of the community, as that of the banking system, the great majority of the people will discover its evils, if any, and that our legislators will, from time to time, correct such errors and imperfections as experience shall dictate. As a general principle, the compiler is in favour of such a system as, on the one hand, will induce that class of community who do not wish to use their money in the way of active business, to vest the same in some safe institution, where, for a reasonable interest, the industrious and enterprising class of community, can be furnished with a capital that will enable them either to commence or increase their business to advantage; and on the other hand, supply the community with a safe and sound circulating medium. One of the objects, and one of the consequences of banks is, to bring into active circulation, at a reasonable interest, certain moneyed capital, which would otherwise, in a great measure, lie dormant. There is no fixed rule for the precise amount of moneyed capital that may be beneficially employed, both to the lender and borrower; but it may be laid down as an elementary rule, that, under a wise and judicious system of laws, a reasonable supply of moneyed capital tends, not only to bring into successful operation, and to increase the productive labour of a country, but to furnish a ready market for the fruits of such productive labour, and thereby produce an approximation to an equality of wealth, and of all the comforts of life.

That there may be some evils of minor consideration in the whole range of the banking system, will not be denied: and where, let it be asked, did there ever exist a great good without a real, or at least, a fancied concomitant evil? Should we discard every operation but that which is free from real or fancied imperfections, civil society would be at a stand, and all intercourse between man and man would necessarily be severed: the bare idea of such a state of things is too insignificant to merit discussion: as a general rule, we may safely act upon the principle, that in any public or private transaction, we will thoroughly and candidly consider the probable good and the probable evil that may arise from the measure. Should it contain such principles as are in themselves evidently judicious and lawful, and nothing of a pernicious, immoral, or unlawful tendency, any one

other kinds of produce or merchandise. This is
nothing more nor less than the vicissitudes of trade,

---

would be justifiable, upon any principle whatever, in engaging
in the undertaking, notwithstanding some serious consequences, beyond the bounds of probability, *might arise* out
of it.
 These remarks are made from the fact, that a number of
political leaders, and editors of newspapers, are continually
pointing out in the banking system, not only existing evils,
which, it is believed, their imaginations only have led them
to discover, but others, which, under our present government,
and as banks are now constituted, never have, and never can
arise. Among other devices, the passions and the prejudices
of the poor, and of the labouring classes are appealed to, and
an attempt made to convince them, that the principle of banking is calculated to create an aristocracy, and a state of
things unfriendly and injurious to their interests and liberties. A moment's reflection only upon the manner in which
banks are constituted, will show the fallacy of such pretensions; and if experience be any test, it can be shown that if
this doctrine be true, that there are aristocratic cartmen,
aristocratic day labourers, aristocratic seamen, aristocratic
widows, and aristocratic orphans. Wealth, it is admitted,
ever has had, and ever will have, in all countries, its natural
influence; but no reasonable man, it is presumed, will pretend, that any one owning a thousand dollars in bank stock,
possesses a greater influence than if he had the same in
houses, lands, or any thing else convertible into money. The
compiler of this work is a poor man! he has nothing except
what he receives from his daily exertions, and if he knows
his own mind, he possesses a feeling in common for the best
interests of the labouring class of community; he has never
been oppressed by banks, nor has he any fears upon that
head. On the contrary, the compiler can confidently say,
that so far as his own experience extends, he has ever found,
that when there was the greatest circulation of money, he
could the most easily obtain a livelihood; and it is to be regretted, that in this country, there are a class of political
leaders who, under the plausible pretence of being friendly to
the poor, are attempting to influence them against measures
in which their best interests are identified; and it is to be
doubly regretted, from the circumstance that this class of
political leaders do not themselves believe what they pretend;
and often, in private circles, exult that they can carry the

arising from various causes, over which it is impossible to always have a complete control.

Now, suppose that there were in the United States six hundred Presidents, without a single customer or dependent secured by law. Suppose, also, that each was so situated that he could not gain even such a supporter or customer as is created by mutual dependence, except by his industry and integrity: will any one pretend that such Presidents would possess a dangerous influence? The idea is too preposterous, and all that need to be said is, that if such men possess a dangerous influence, then every sober, discreet, and industrious farmer possesses a dangerous influence. Indeed, upon that principle, a dangerous influence pervades the whole industry of the country, farmers, mechanics, and all.

In conclusion, the compiler feels it due to himself, in order that he may not be misunderstood, to make an explanation, as to any thing that may have the appearance of personality, and particularly as respects President Jackson. The compiler does not know that personage, only by reputation; and it is presumed, that he does not know that there is such a person as the compiler of this work. No favour was ever, directly or indirectly, asked of him by the compiler, and none ever was, or ever is, expected. President Jackson, as is well understood, is no longer before the American public as a candidate for their suffrages; and, according to the natural course of human events, must soon appear

---

rabble, as they are pleased to term a certain class, with them. Whenever the people think and judge for themselves, demagogues do not succeed; and it is to be hoped, that every member of community will consider himself to be one of the number from whom emanates all legitimate authority, and govern himself accordingly.—*Compiler.*

The President shall have Power to fill up all Vacancies that may happen during the Recess of the Senate, by granting Commissions which shall expire at the end of their next Session.[66]

before a higher tribunal than that of the people of the United States; it cannot, therefore, be supposed, that the compiler is influenced by any personal consideration. He expressly disavows any such. It is not *President Jackson,* but it is *some of his measures,* that the compiler has taken the liberty to criticise,—if those measures are sanctioned by the American people, they afford a precedent equal in force and authority to a conceded right, which successors to the presidency, less patriotic than President Jackson, may exercise injuriously to the best interests of the people. The great popularity which President Jackson has heretofore sustained may induce the remainder of his friends, from generous feelings, to support measures which, if personal considerations were out of view, they would condemn. They should, however, follow the example of a number of our most worthy and patriotic citizens, who were the first and early friends of President Jackson, but who now consider that the time has arrived when the love of country should triumph over every other consideration.

66. The Senate by a decision of April 20, 1822, seem distinctly to have held, that the President could not create the office of minister, and make appointments to such an office during the recess, without the consent of the senate. By "vacancies" they understood to be meant vacancies occurring from death, resignation, promotion, or removal. The word "happen" had relation to some casualty, not provided for by law. If the senate

SECTION 3. He shall from time to time give to the Congress Information of the State of the Union, and recommend to their Consideration such Measures as he shall judge necessary and expedient ;[67] he may, on extraordinary Occasions, convene both Houses, or either of them, and in case of Disagreement between them, with Respect to the Time of Adjournment, he may adjourn them to such Time as he shall think proper ;[68] he shall receive Ambassadors

are in session, when offices are created by law, which have not as yet been filled, and nominations are not then made to them by the President, he cannot appoint to such offices during the recess of the senate ; because the vacancy does not happen during the recess. In many instances, where offices are created by law, special power is on this very account given to the President to fill them during the recess.—*Story's Com. v.* 3, *p.* 411, 412.

67. From the nature and duties of the executive department, he must possess more extensive sources of information, as well as in regard to *domestic* as *foreign* affairs, than can belong to congress. The true workings of the laws ; the defects in the nature or arrangement of the general system of trade, finance, and justice ; and the military, naval, and civil establishments of the union, are more readily seen, and more constantly under the view of the executive, than they can possibly be of any other department.—*Story's Com. v.* 3, *p.* 413.

68. The power to convene congress on extraordinary occasions is indispensable to the proper operations and even safety of the government. The

and other public Ministers;[60] he shall take
Care that the Laws be faithfully execu-

power to adjourn congress in cases of disagreement is equally indispensable; since it is the only
peaceable way of terminating a controversy, which
can lead to nothing but distraction in the public
councils.—*Story's Com. v.* 3, *p.* 413, 414.

A discussion was carried on this season (1833–4)
through the newspapers, involving the right of the
President to adjourn both houses in case one house
only had legislated upon the subject. One party
maintained that if the house of representatives
should, by resolution, fix upon a day for adjournment, send the resolution to the senate for concurrence, and the senate should not act upon the
subject, by the time fixed for adjournment, that
such *non-action* would be tantamount to a *non-
concurrence* or disagreement with the house, and
that the President in consequence of such *non-action*
would have the same right to adjourn both houses,
as though the senate had legislated upon the subject, and, in formal act disagreed with the house.
The other party insisted that no disagreement
could exist until both houses had legislated upon
the subject. The latter position seems to be the
more conformable to the views of Judge Story, as
above expressed, to reason, and to common sense.
—*Compiler.*

69. A government may in its discretion lawfully
refuse to receive an ambassador, or other minister,
without its affording any just cause of war. But
it would generally be deemed an unfriendly act,
and might provoke hostilities, unless accompanied
by conciliatory explanations.—*Story's Com. v.* 3,
p. 415.

ted,[70] and shall Commission all the Officers of the United States.

70. The duty imposed upon the President, "to take care that the laws be faithfully executed, follows out the strong injunctions of his office, that he will" preserve, protect, and defend the Constitution.—*Story's Com. v. 3. p.* 414.

President Jackson, in his proclamation of the 10th of December, 1832, laconically says, " The laws of the United States must be executed. I have no discretionary powers on the subject. My duty is emphatically pronounced in the Constitution!" From these sound and just views of President Jackson, it is fair to infer, that whatever law may have been passed by Congress, whether it be expedient or inexpedient; just or unjust; constitutional or unconstitutional; it is his duty, until such law be either repealed, or pronounced by the Judiciary to be unconstitutional, to take care that the same be faithfully executed.—*Compiler.*

The President cannot be liable to arrest, imprisonment, or detention, while he is in the discharge of the duties of his office; and for this purpose, his person must be deemed, in civil cases at least, to possess an official inviolability. In the exercise of his political powers, he is to use his own discretion, and is accountable only to his country and his own conscience. But he has no authority to control other officers of the government in relation to the duties imposed upon them by law.—*Story's Com. v. 3. p.* 419.

The question as to the extent of the rights, powers, and duties of the President, in ordering, controlling, or directing the officers of government, in the discharge of the duties, assigned them by law, has of late, become a topic of so warm and animated discussion through the public prints, that the compiler has thought proper to bestow, in addition to the views of the learned commentator upon the subject, a few remarks of his own. In order to arrive at a just comprehension of the subject, it is necessary that we clearly ascertain the rights, powers, and duties of the President, in relation to officers of government, as also the responsibility, or accountability of officers of government, either to the President, to congress, or to the public, as defined and prescribed by the constitution and the laws of the United States. The following extract from a decision of the Supreme Court of the United States, in a case of Marbury vs. Madison, then Secretary of State, on an application for a mandamus, requiring the defendant, Mr. Madison, to deliver the plaintiff a certain commission, which was withheld from the plaintiff by the defendant, and which was signed by John Adams, President of the United States, appointing the plaintiff justice of the peace for the District of Columbia, for the term of five years, will tend to elucidate the principle.

"By the Constitution of the United States, the President is invested with certain important political powers, in the exercise of which he is to use his own discretion, and is accountable only to his country in his political character, and to his own conscience. To aid him in the performance of these duties, he is authorized to appoint certain officers, who act by his authority and in conformity with his orders. In such cases, their acts are his acts, and whatever opinion may be entertained of the manner in which executive discretion may be used, still there exists, and can exist, no power, to control that discretion. The subjects are political. They respect the nation, not individual rights; and being intrusted to the executive, the decision of the executive is conclusive. The application of this remark will be perceived by adverting to the act of Congress for establishing the department of Foreign Affairs. This officer, as his duties were prescribed by that act, is to conform precisely to the will of the President. He is the mere organ by whom that will is communicated. The acts of such an officer, as an officer, can never be examinable by the Courts. But when the Legislature proceeds to impose on that officer *other* duties; when he is directed peremptorily to perform certain other acts; when the rights of individuals are dependent on the performance of those acts; he is so far the officer of the law; is amenable to the laws for his conduct; and cannot, at his discretion, sport away the vested rights of others.

The conclusion from this reasoning is, that where the heads of departments are the political or confidential agents of the executive, merely to execute the will of the President, or rather to act in cases in which the executive possesses a constitutional or legal discretion, nothing can be more perfectly clear than that their acts are only politically examinable.

But where a *specific duty* is assigned by law, and individual rights depend upon the performance of that duty, it seems equally clear that the individual who considers himself injured, has a right to resort to the laws of his country for remedy.—*Cranch's Rep. vol.* 1, *p.* 165, 166.

By the 2d section of the 2d article of the Constitution, it is declared, that the President shall be Commander-in-Chief of the Army and Navy of the United States, and of the Militia of the several States, when called into the actual service of the United States. By the same section it is declared, that " he (the President) shall have power, by and with the advice and consent of the Senate, to make treaties."

For the purpose of carrying into effect these provisions of the Constitution, Congress on the 27th of July, 1789, passed an act for establishing an Executive Department, to be denominated the " Department of Foreign Affairs." (By an act of Sept. 15th 1789, the title of " Department of State" was substituted for that of " Department of Foreign Affairs,") which, among other duties requires, that the Secretary " shall perform and execute such duties as shall, from time to time, be enjoined on or intrusted to him, *by the President of the United States*, agreeable to the Constitution, relative to correspondences, commissions, or instructions, to or with public ministers or consuls, from the United States, or to negotiations with public ministers from Foreign States or princes, or to memorials, or other applications from foreign public ministers, or other foreigners, or to such other matters *respecting foreign affairs, as the President of the United States shall assign to the said Department.*" On the 7th August, 1789, an act was passed, establishing the Department of War; and on the 30th of April, 1798, an act was passed, establishing the Department of the Navy. The provisions of both these acts require the Secretary of each Department, like that of the Secretary of the Department of State, to execute such *orders as he shall receive, from the President of the United States.* It is perfectly clear, from the provisions contained in the Constitution, and from the aforementioned acts of Congress, that in certain cases they require the Secretary, *not to execute any specific duties prescribed by law,* but, to aid and assist the President, as occasion may require, in such transactions, as, by the Constitution, are intrusted to his discretion. The very terms of the Constitution, and of the acts of Congress in relation thereto, are such, that no act of Congress prescribing any specific duties, where discretionary power must necessarily be exercised, could, from the nature of the duties to be performed, be carried into effect. A law moreover of that kind would, in most cases, be an assumption of executive duties. In conducting negotiations, making treaties, &c., there can be no doubt but the President has the right to prescribe, order, or direct, any thing in relation to the same: as much so, as a merchant has to order and direct his clerk in his mercantile transactions. It is also clear, that the acts of the Secretary are not his own acts, but those of the President; for which the President is accountable to his country.

By reference to the statute books, it will be perceived that in several other acts of Congress, specific duties are assigned to certain officers of government, under the direction of the President of the United States. Congress in framing particular laws have, without doubt, taken into view the most competent head, to whom their supervision, with the greatest public advantage, may be intrusted; and in all cases where any national object is to be carried into effect, and where the act of Congress for that purpose expressly directs that it be " under the direction of the President of the United States," there can be no doubt but that the executive has a right to give any officer, intrusted by law, with its execution, such lawful orders and directions as he may think proper.

Having established, as the compiler humbly conceives, beyond the shadow of doubt, the right of the President to control those appointed by law, to aid and assist him in certain transactions intrusted to his discretion, as also those whose specific duties are by law subject to his supervision,—we proceed in the next place to show, from certain acts of Congress, the inference to be equally conclusive, that in certain, if not in all cases, where specific duties are assigned by law to an officer appointed by the government, and where *such officer is not expressly required, by law, to execute the trust reposed in him, under " the direction of the President of the United States,"* the executive has no more constitutional right to interfere with, or control him, in the lawful discharge of his duties; than such an officer has a right to interfere with the President, in the discharge of his official duties. Each has his duties prescribed by the Constitution and laws; and each, for the sake of preserving that almost inimitable harmony, planned by the skilful architects that framed our excellent Constitution, must move in his own orbit. A case in which the President has no right to order, control, or dictate to, a public officer, is found in the 1st and 2d section of the act of September 2d, 1789, to establish a Treasury Department, which is in the words following:

1. " Be it enacted, &c., That there shall be a department of treasury, in which shall be the following officers, namely; a Secretary of the Treasury, to be deemed head of the department; a comptroller, an auditor, a treasurer, a register, and an assistant to the secretary of the treasury, which assistant shall be appointed by the said secretary.

2. " That it shall be the duty of the Secretary of the Treasury to digest and prepare plans for the improvement and management of the revenue, and for the support of public credit; to prepare and report estimates of the public revenue, and the public expenditures; to

superintend the collection of the revenue; to decide on the form of keeping and stating accounts and making returns, and to grant, under the limitations herein established, or to be hereafter provided, all warrants for moneys to be issued from the treasury, in pursuance of appropriations by law; to execute such services relative to the sale of the lands belonging to the United States, *as may be by law required of him;* to make report, and give information, to either branch of the legislature, in person or in writing, (as he may be required) respecting all matters referred to him by the Senate or House of Representatives, or which shall appertain to his office; and generally, to perform all such services, relative to the finances, as he shall be directed to perform."

This act, and that for establishing the Department of State, were both passed during the first session of the first Congress held under the Constitution, in which body, were a large number of the framers of that instrument. The act for establishing the Treasury Department, as will be perceived, was passed subsequently to that for the Department of Foreign Affairs, and for the Department of War. The reader will also observe, that the duties of the Secretary of either the latter, is to be performed *under the direction of the President of the United States.*—While in the former, no such phrase, nor anything tantamount thereto, either expressed or implied, is to be found in the whole act. The same, as respects the Post Office Department, the first clause of the first section of the act establishing which says, " That there be established at the seat of the government of the United States, a general Post Office, *under the direction of the Post Master General.*" Other officers, whose duties are similar to those of the Secretary of the Treasury and of the Post Master General, might be mentioned; but it is presumed that these are sufficient to clearly establish the principle, that where specific duties are assigned to an officer of government, and where express authority to control the officer is not given the executive in the act of Congress assigning such duties to the officer,—the President has no constitutional right to interfere with such an officer in the lawful discharge of his duty, as prescribed by law. Were such an executive right once established, the effect would be, to take away all responsibility of the officer, and vest in one man, the whole control of the multifarious duties, assigned by law, to every officer of government. It may be worthy of further remark, that not only are *specific* duties assigned by law to the Secretary of the Treasury, but also *discretionary powers*. As for example; the Secretary of the Treasury, by authority vested in him by the act of March, 3d, 1797, is authorized under certain circumstances, to mitigate or remit fines, penalties, forfeitures, or disabilities. He is also empowered, by the 16th section of the Charter of the Bank of the United States, to withhold the public deposits from that institution. From an examination of both of these acts, it will be clearly perceived, that Congress in framing the laws, *contemplated not any specific duties to be performed, but certain exigencies requiring the exercise of discretionary powers*. These discretionary powers were unqualifiedly vested by law, in the Secretary of the Treasury, for which he is accountable only *to Congress*.

By so doing, Congress without doubt had in view the preservation of one of the leading objects of the framers of our system of government, which was to avoid, on the one hand, too great a concentration of power in the hands of the executive, and on the other, to secure a rigid accountability of all the officers of government.— For the purpose of insuring such responsibility, the 4th section of the second article of the constitution declares that, "the President, Vice President, *and all other civil officers of the United States* shall be removed from office, on impeachment for, and conviction of, treason, bribery, or other high crimes and misdemeanours." Should the Secretary of the Treasury abuse the trust reposed in him, the House of Representatives would have the right, and it would be their solemn duty, as the guardians of the rights of the people, to prefer articles of impeachment against him.

Again:—By the 23d section of the Bank Charter already alluded to, it is provided, that whenever " the *President of the United States* shall have reason to believe, that the Charter has been violated, it may be lawful for congress to direct, or *the President to order* a *scire facias* to be sued out of the Circuit Court of the district of Pennsylvania, &c." Here we find that certain discretionary powers are vested in the President, and in the same act of Congress, certain other discretionary powers, in the Secretary of the Treasury.

From these provisions of the act, we arrive at the conclusion, that not only the President, but also the Secretary of the Treasury, is each required to attend to the discretionary powers, assigned to him by law. This is the only rational construction, that, from the terms of the act can be given,—any other would involve one in the novel and extraordinary position, that the terms of the act, have no definitely literal meaning, or that although Congress has expressly assigned certain discretionary duties to the Secretary of the Treasury, still these discretionary duties are not vested in him, but in the President,—a position which it is believed, needs only to be mentioned, that it may be unqualifiedly condemned.

The nature of our government is such, that the people's representatives should be extremely watchful in not permitting the President, whilst exercising his legitimate authority, to encroach, by way of forced construction, or under plausible pretexts, upon the powers and duties of others. These remarks are suggested from a question frequently proposed, whether the President has a right to remove an officer of government, who does not obey his orders in relation to any specific duties reposed in him by law,—to which it may be answered, that for a palpable neglect by an officer of any specific duties, prescribed by law, or for a wanton abuse of his office, for improper and unlawful purposes, there can be no doubt but that the President, agreeably to the construction given by the first Congress as to the power of removals, would have a right to displace such officer, and appoint another for the time being. But where an officer faithfully attends to the *specific* duties of his office, or when he is vested with discretionary authority, as in the case mentioned in relation to the Secretary of the Treasury, it is equally clear, particularly in the exercise of a discretionary power, be the officer right or wrong, that the President has no authority to control him.

The compiler feels confident of the correctness of this principle, not only from the genius of our government, but also from the several acts of Congress vesting discretionary powers in certain officers of government, and the usages of the executive in relation thereto, from the first organization of our government until a recent period. Nor is it to be inferred that because the President has *the right of removal*, his functions are in any way enlarged on that account. The President, it is true, might say to an officer of government, that if he did not execute the duties of his office as *he* directed, he should be removed from office ; so might he intimate to one that if he did not commit a felony, or some other atrocious act, that he should be displaced : but such an act would clearly be a wanton abuse of power, for which a Congress of the United States, unless faithless to the trust reposed in them, would prefer articles of impeachment against the executive. Some have argued that the clause in the constitution requiring the President, " to take care the laws be faithfully executed," gives him the unqualified right to order, control, or direct all officers appointed by the government. In answer to such a position it may be observed, that in nearly, or quite all our State constitutions there is a like provision, requiring the executive " to take care that the laws be faithfully executed," and that in several States, the Governor, like the President, has the right of nomination. If, then, this is an incidental right of the President, arising from the right to nominate, and the consequent right to remove, the principle is equally applicable to the executive of several of the State governments, a right which it is believed no executive ever thought of assuming. In the State of New-York, sheriffs and clerks of counties, are chosen by the people ; but the right to remove them, in certain cases, is more fully and distinctly conferred by the constitution on its executive, than that by the constitution of the United States, on

SECTION 4. The President, Vice-President and all Civil Officers of the United States,[71] shall be removed from Office on Impeachment for, and Conviction of, Treason, Bribery, or other high Crimes and Misdemeanours.

the President, to remove the United States officers. In the former the express right is given by the constitution of New York; in the latter, the right is only given by a forced construction of the constitution of the United States. The existing constitution of the State of New York has been in operation twelve years; the sheriffs and clerks of counties are State officers, and have specific duties assigned them by law, but no one it is believed has ever known or heard of the executive having attempted to order, direct, or control a sheriff or clerk in the discharge of his duties except it were in cases expressly warranted by law; the people it is believed would not submit to such an indignity and usurpation of power *by their Governor*, and it is to be hoped, that should the *President* ever assume to himself powers not delegated by the constitution and laws, that there will be found in the house of representatives, a sufficient number, who, instead of being slaves to party or to power, will be so far influenced by the solemn obligation of their oaths, as to bring the usurper to a just punishment.—*Compiler*.

71. All officers of the United States who hold their appointments under the national government, whether these duties are executive or judicial, in the highest or in the lowest departments of government, with the exception of officers in the army and navy, are properly civil officers within the meaning of the constitution, and liable to impeachment, *Story's Com. v.* 2, *p.* 258.

ARTICLE III.

SECTION 1. The Judicial Power of the United States, shall be vested in one Supreme Court,[73] and in such inferior Courts as the

Judiciary.

72. The constitution has wisely established, that there shall be one Supreme Court, with a view to uniformity of decision in all cases whatsoever, belonging to the judicial department, whether they arise at the common law or in equity, or within the admiralty or prize jurisdiction; whether they respect the doctrines of mere municipal law, or constitutional law, or the law of nations.—*Story's Com. v. 3, p.* 454.

The theory, neither of the British nor the state constitutions authorizes the revisal of a *judicial sentence by a legislative* act. A legislature, without exceeding its province, cannot reverse a determination, once made in a particular case, though it may prescribe a *new rule, for future cases.*—*Story's Com. v. 3, p.* 445.

On the first organization of the Supreme Court, its judges were of opinion, that from a fair construction of the constitution, their duties were exclusively confined to those appertaining to the Supreme Court, and that it would be incompatible with their judicial duties to officiate in other Courts. They were however required, by the act establishing the judiciary, to perform the duties of Circuit Judges in Circuit Courts. In 1803, it was made a question in the Supreme Court, whether its judges could constitutionally perform circuit duties, and it was decided, that as each member of

Congress may from time to time ordain and establish.[73] The Judges both of the supreme

that body had, in turn, from the commencement of the government, performed circuit duties, the practice could not be safely shaken.—*Story's Com. v. 3, p. 437.*

73. In regard to the power of constituting inferior courts of the Union, it is evidently calculated to obviate the necessity of having recourse to the Supreme Court in every case of federal cognizance. It enables the national government to institute, or authorize, in each state or district of the United States a tribunal competent to the determination of all matters of national jurisdiction within its limits. One of two courses only could be open for adoption; either to create inferior courts under the national authority, to reach all cases fit for the national jurisdiction, which either constitutionally, or conveniently, could not be of original cognizance in the Supreme Court; or to confide jurisdiction of the same cases to the State Courts, with a right of appeal to the Supreme Court. To the latter course solid objections were thought to apply, which rendered it inelligible and unsatisfactory. In the first place, the judges of the State Courts, would be wholly irresponsible to the national government for their conduct in the administration of national justice; so that the national government would, or might be, wholly dependent upon the good will, or sound discretion of the States, in regard to the efficiency, promptitude, and ability, with which the judicial authority of the nation was administered. In the next place, the prevalency of a local, or sectional spirit might be found to disqualify the State tribunals, for a suitable discharge of national judicial functions, and the very modes of appointment

of some of the State judges might render them improper channels of the judicial authority of the Union.

State judges holding their office during pleasure, or from year to year, or for other short periods, would, or at least might, be too little independent to be relied upon for an inflexible execution of the national laws.—*Story's Com. v.* 3, *p.* 447, 448.

It would be difficult, and perhaps not desirable, to lay down any general rules in relation to the cases, in which the judicial power of the Courts of the United States, is exclusive of the State Courts, or in which it may be made so by Congress, until they shall be settled by some positive adjudication of the Supreme Court.—*Story's Com. v.* 3, *p.* 621.

In regard to jurisdiction over crimes committed against the authority of the United States, it has been held, that no part of the jurisdiction can, consistently with the Constitution, be delegated to State tribunals. It is true that Congress has in various acts, conferred the right to prosecute for offences, penalties, and forfeitures, in the State Courts. But the latter have in many instances, declined the jurisdiction, and asserted its unconstitutionality. And certainly there is, at the present time, a decided preponderance of judicial authority in the State Courts against the authority of Congress to confer the power.—*Story's Com. v.* 3, *p.* 624.

Under the power granted to erect tribunals, inferior to the Supreme Court, Congress have established thirty-two *District Courts*, and seven *Circuit Courts*.

To each of the *District Courts*, a District Judge is appointed. The Circuit Court extends to several District Courts, and is held by a District Judge, and one of the Judges of the Supreme Court, and, under special circumstances, the Supreme Court may assign two of its body to attend a Circuit Court.—*Compiler.*

The *Circuit Courts* have *original* and *exclusive* cognizance (except in particular cases) of all crimes and offences cognizable under the authority of the United States, exceeding the degree of ordinary misdemeanours; and of those they have *concurrent* jurisdiction with the District Courts. They have original cognizance *concurrently* with the Courts of the several States, of all suits of a civil nature at law or in equity, where the matter in dispute exceeds five hundred dollars, and the United States are *plaintiffs*, or an alien is a party, or the suit is between a citizen of the state where it is brought, and a citizen of another state. The Circuit Courts have also original jurisdiction in equity and at law, of all suits arising under the acts of Congress relative to copy-rights, and the rights growing out of patents for new inventions and discoveries in the useful arts.

The Circuit Courts have *appellate* jurisdiction in all final decrees and judgments of the District Courts, where the matter in dispute exceeds fifty dollars.

The *District Courts* have *exclusively* of the State Courts, cognizance of all lesser crimes and offences cognizable under the authority of the United States, and committed either within their respective districts, or upon the high seas, and which are punishable by fine not exceeding one hundred dollars; and imprisonment, not exceeding six months. They have also exlusive *original* cognizance of all civil causes of admiralty and maritime jurisdiction; of seizures under the imposts, navigation, and trade laws of the United States, where the seizures are made on the high seas, or in waters within their respective districts, navigable from the sea by vessels of ten or more tons burden; and of all other seizures under the laws of the United States; and of all suits for penalties, or forfeitures incurred under those laws.—*Compiler.*

Appellate Jurisdiction.

It has never been decided by the Supreme Court whether Courts held by a Justice of Peace, appointed by the President and Senate, are inferior Courts, within the meaning of the Constitution.—*Story's Com. v. 3, p. 497.*

The judges appointed in the territories of the United States are not such judges of inferior Courts, as are contemplated by the Constitution. The jurisdiction with which they are invested is not a part of the judicial powers, which is defined in the third article of the Constitution; but arises from the same general sovereignty. Congress may, therefore, rightfully limit the tenure of offices of the judges of the territorial Courts, as well as their jurisdiction; and it has been accordingly limited to a short period of years.—*Story's Com. v. 3, p. 499.*

The most usual modes of exercising appellate jurisdiction, at least those, which are most known in the United States, are by writ of error, or by an appeal, or by some process of removal of a suit from an inferior tribunal. *An appeal* is a process of civil law origin, and removes a cause, entirely subjecting the fact, as well as the law, to a review and a retrial. A *writ of error*, is a process of common law origin, and it removes nothing for re-examination, but the law. The *former mode* is usually adopted in cases of equity and admiralty jurisdiction; the latter in suits at common law tried by a jury.—*Story's Com. v. 3, p. 627.*

[For further information as to the extent of the

and inferior Courts, shall hold their Offices during good Behaviour,[74] and shall, at stated

powers and duties of the several Courts, the reader is referred to Story's Commentaries, Kent's Commentaries, Duer's Outlines, or to the Laws of the United States.]—*Compiler.*

74. The standard of good behaviour, for the continuance in office of the judicial magistracy, is certainly one of the most valuable of the modern improvements in the practice of government. In a *monarchy*, it is an excellent barrier to the despotism of the prince; in a *republic*, it is a no less excellent barrier to the encroachments and oppressions of the representative body. And it is the best expedient which can be devised in any government, to secure a steady, upright, and impartial administration of the laws.—*Story's Com. v. 3, p. 458.*

That inflexible and uniform adherence to the rights of the Constitution, and of individuals, which we perceive to be indispensable in the Courts of justice, can certainly not be expected from judges, who hold their offices by a temporary commission. Periodical appointments, however regulated, or by whomsoever made, would, in some way or other, be fatal to their necessary independence. For any corrupt violation or omission of the trusts confided to the judges, they are liable to be impeached, and upon conviction removed from office. The executive not only dispenses the *honours*, but holds the sword of the community. The *legislature* not only commands the *purse*, but prescribes the rules by which the duties and rights of every citizen are to be regulated. The *judiciary*, on the contrary, has no influence over the *sword*, or the *purse*, no direction either of the strength, or of the wealth of the society; and can take no active

Times, receive for their Services, a Compensation, which shall not be diminished during their Continuance in Office.[75]

SECTION 2. The Judicial Power shall extend to all Cases, in Law and Equity, arising under this Constitution,[76] the Laws of the United States,[77] and Treaties made, or which shall be

resolution whatever.—*Story's Com. v. 3, p. 458, 462.*

Salary.

75. Next to permanency in office, nothing can contribute more to the independence of the judges, than a fixed provision for their support. The remark made in relation to the President is equally applicable here. In the general course of human nature *a power over a man's subsistence amounts to a power over his will.*—*Story's Com. v. 3, p. 490.*

76. Mr. Chief Justice Jay, in his very able opinion in *Chisholm* vs. *the State of Georgia*, has drawn up a summary of the more general reasoning on which each of the delegations of power is founded.

First, *To all cases arising under this Constitution.*—Because the meaning, construction, and operation of a compact ought always to be ascertained by all the parties, not by authority derived only from one of them.

77. Second, *To all cases arising under the laws of the United States.*—Because, as such laws, constitutionally made, are obligatory on each State, the measure of obligation and obedience ought not to be decided and fixed by the party, from whom they are

made, under their Authority;[78]—to all Cases
affecting Ambassadors, other public Ministers
and Consuls;[79]—to all cases of admiralty and
maritime Jurisdiction;[80]—to Controversies to
which the United States shall be a party;[81]—to
Controversies between two or more States;[82]

due, but from a tribunal deriving authority from
both the parties.

78. Third, *To all cases arising under treaties
made by their authority.*—Because as treaties are
compacts made by, and obligatory on, the whole
nation, their operations ought not to be affected, or
regulated by the local laws, or Courts of a part of the
nation.

79. Fourth, *To all cases affecting ambassadors,
or other public ministers and consuls.*—Because, as
these are officers of foreign nations, whom this nation are bound to protect, and treat according to
the laws of nations, cases affecting them ought
only to be cognizable by national authority.

80. Fifth, *To all cases of admiralty and maratime
jurisdiction.*—Because, as the seas are the joint property of nations, whose rights and privileges relative thereto, are regulated by the law of nations
and treaties, such cases necessarily belong to the
national jurisdiction.

81. Sixth, *To controversies to which the United
States shall be a party.*—Because in cases, in which
the whole people are interested, it would not be
equal, or wise, to let any one State, decide, and
measure out the justice due to others.

82. Seventh, *To controversies between two or more
States.*—Because domestic tranquillity requires,
that the contentions of States should be peaceably
terminated by a common judicatory; and, because,

—between a State and Citizens of another State ;[83]—between Citizens of different States,*—between Citizens of the same State claiming lands under Grants of different States,[84] and between a State, or the Citizens thereof, and foreign States, Citizens or Subjects.†[85]

in a free country, justice ought not to depend on the *will* of either litigants.

83. Eighth, *To controversies between a State and citizen of another State.*—Because in case a State (that is all the citizens of it) has demands against some citizens of another State, it is better, that she should prosecute their demands in a national Court, than in a Court of the State, to which those citizens belong; the danger of irritation and criminations, arising from apprehensions and suspicions of partiality, being thereby obviated. Because, in cases, where some citizens of one State have demands against all the citizens of another State, the cause of liberty and the rights of men forbid, that the latter should be the sole judges of the justice due to the latter; and true republican government requires, that free and equal citizens should have free, fair, and equal justice.

84. Ninth, *To controversies between citizens of the same State, claiming lands under grants of different States.*—Because as the rights of the two States to grant the land are drawn into question, neither of the two States ought to decide the controversy.

85. Tenth, *To controversies between a State,* or

---

* A citizen of the District of Columbia, is not a citizen of a State within the meaning of the Constitution of the United States—*Hepburn et al* vs. *Ellzey,* 2 *Cranch,* 445.

† See a restriction of this provision. Amendments, art. 11.

In all Cases affecting Ambassadors, other public Ministers and Consuls, and those in which a State shall be Party, the Supreme Court shall have original Jurisdiction.[86] In all the other Cases before mentioned, the Supreme Court shall have appellate Jurisdiction, both as to Law and Fact, with such Exceptions, and under such Regulations as the Congress shall make.*[87]

the citizens thereof, and foreign states, citizens, or subjects; Because as every nation is responsible for the conduct of its citizens towards other nations, all questions touching the justice due to foreign nations, or people, ought to be ascertained by, and depend on, national authority.—*Story's Com. v.* 3, *p.* 499, 500, 501, 502.

We are to understand the phrase, " all cases in law and equity," to mean *criminal*, as well as *civil* cases; also those in which the English common law governs, and is to be recognised by the court. Any question in relation to the constitution, laws, and treaties of the United States, and submitted to the courts by a party, is a case.—*Story's Com. v.* 3, *p.* 502. 506, 507.

86. Congress cannot constitutionally confer on any court, other than the Supreme Court, original jurisdiction in cases affecting ambassadors and other public ministers, consuls, and where a state is a party.

87. Neither can they confer upon the Supreme

---

* The appellate jurisdiction of the Supreme Court of the United States extends to a final judgment or decree in any suit in the highest court of law, or equity of a state, where is drawn in question the validity of a treaty, &c. *Martin* vs. *Hunter's lessee,* 1 *Wheaton,* 304.

Court original jurisdiction (excepting in the enumerated cases,) but congress may vest the same in

---

Such judgment, &c. may be re-examined by writ of error, in the same manner as if rendered in a Circuit Court. *Ib.*

If the cause has been once remanded before, and the State Court decline or refuse to carry into effect the mandate of the Supreme Court thereon, this Court will proceed to a final decision of the same, and award execution thereon.

Quære.—Whether this Court has authority to issue a mandamus to the State Court to enforce a former judgment? *Ib.* 362.

If the validity or construction of a treaty of the United States is drawn in question, and the decision is against its validity, or the title specially set up by either party under the treaty, this Court has jurisdiction to ascertain that title, and determine its legal validity, and is not confined to the abstract construction of the treaty itself. *Ib.* 362.

Quære.—Whether the Courts of the United States have jurisdiction of offences at common law against the United States? *United States* vs. *Coolidge*, 1 *Wheaton*, 415.

The Courts of the United States have exclusive jurisdiction of all seizures made on land or water for a breach of the laws of the United States, and any intervention of a State authority, which by taking the thing seized out of the hands of the United States' officer, might obstruct the exercise of this jurisdiction, is illegal. *Slocum* vs. *Mayberry et al*, 2 *Wheaton*, 1. 9.

In such a case the Court of the United States have cognizance of the seizure, may enforce a re-delivery of the thing by attachment or other summary process. *Ib.* 9.

The question under such a seizure, whether a forfeiture has been actually incurred, belongs exclusively to the Courts of the United States, and it depends upon the final decree of such Courts, whether the seizure is to be deemed rightful or tortious. *Ib.* 9, 10.

If the seizing officer refuses to institute proceedings to ascertain the forfeiture, the District Court may, on application of the aggrieved party, compel the officer to proceed to adjudication, or to abandon the seizure. *Ib.* 10.

The jurisdiction of the Circuit Court of the United States extends to a case between citizens of Kentucky, claiming lands exceeding the value of five hundred dollars, under any inferior court established by the United States.—*Story's Com. v. 3, p.* 573, 574.

different grants, the one issued by the state of Kentucky, and the other by the state of Virginia, upon warrants issued by Virginia, and locations founded thereon, prior to the separation of Kentucky from Virginia. It is the grant which passes the *legal* title to the land, and if the controversy is founded upon the conflicting grants of different States, the judicial power of the Courts of the United States extends to the case, whatever may have been the equitable title of the parties prior to the grant. *Colson et al* vs. *Lewis,* 2 *Wheaton,* 377.

Under the judiciary of 1789, ch. 20, sec. 25, giving appellate jurisdiction to the Supreme Court of the United States, from the final judgment or decree of the highest court of law or equity of a State, in certain cases the writ of error may be directed to any court in which the record and judgment on which it is to act may be found; and if the record has been remitted by the highest court, &c. to another court of the state, it may be brought by the writ of error from that court. *Gelston* vs. *Hoyt,* 3 *Wheaton,* 246. 303.

The remedies in the Courts of the United States at common law and in ceuity are to be, not according to the practice of state courts, but according to the principles of common law and equity as defined in England. The doctrine reconciled with the decision of the courts of Tennessee, permitting an equitable title to be asserted in an action at law. *Robinson* vs. *Campbell,* 3 *Wheaton,* 221.

Remedies in respect to real property, are to be pursued according to the *lex loci rei sitac. Id.* 219.

The Courts of the United States have *exclusive* cognizance of questions of forfeiture upon all seizures made under the laws of the United States, and it is not competent for a state court to entertain or decide such question of forfeiture. If a sentence of condemnation be definitively pronounced by the proper Court of the United States, it is conclusive that a forfeiture is incurred : if a sentence of acquittal, it is equally conclusive against the forfeiture, and in either case the question cannot be again litigated in any common law forever. *Gelston* vs. *Hoyt,* 3 *Wheaton,* 246. 311.

Where a seizure is made for a supposed forfeiture under a law of the United States, no action of trespass lies in any common law tribunal, until a final decree is pronounced upon the proceeding *in rem* to enforce such forfeiture ; "for it

The Trial of all Crimes, except in Cases of Impeachment, shall be by Jury; and

---

depends upon the final decree of the Court proceeding *in rem*, whether such seizure is to be deemed rightful or tortious, and the action if brought before such decree is made, is brought too soon. *Id.* 113.

If a suit be brought against the seizing officer for the supposed trespass while the suit for the forfeiture is depending, the fact of such pending may be pleaded in abatement, or as a temporary bar of the action. If after a decree of condemnation, then that fact may be pleaded as a bar: if after an acquittal with a certificate of reasonable cause of seizure, then that may be pleaded as a bar. If after an acquittal without such certificate, then the officer is without any justification for the seizure, and it is definitively settled to be a tortious act. If to an action of trespass in a state court for a seizure, the seizing officer plead the fact of forfeiture in his defence without averring a *lis pendens*, or a condemnation, or an acquittal, with a certificate of reasonable cause of seizure, the plea is bad: for it attempts to put in issue the question of forfeiture in a state court. *Id.* 314.

Supposing that the third article of the Constitution of the United States which declares, that "the judicial power shall extend to all cases of admiralty and maritime jurisdiction" vested in the United States exclusive jurisdiction of all such cases, and that a murder committed in the waters of a state where the tide ebbs and flows, is a case of admiralty and maritime jurisdiction; yet Congress have not in the 8th section of the act of 1790, ch. 9, "for the punishment of certain crimes against the United States," so exercised this power as to confer on the Courts of the U. States urisdiction over such murder. *United States* vs. *Bevans*, 3 *Wheaton*, 336. 387.

Quære.—Whether Courts of common law have concurrent jurisdiction with the admiralty over murder committed in bays, &c. which are enclosed parts of the sea? *Id.* 387.

The grant to the United States in the Constitution of all cases of admiralty and maritime jurisdiction, does not extend to a cession of the waters in which those cases may arise, or of general jurisdiction over the same. Congress may pass all laws which are necessary for giving the most complete effect to the exercise of the admiralty and maritime such Trial shall be held in the State where the said Crimes shall have been commit-

---

jurisdiction granted to the Government of the Union: but the general jurisdiction over the place subject to this grant, adheres to the territory as a portion of territory not yet given away, and the residuary powers of legislation still remain in the state. *Id.* 389.

The Supreme Court of the United States has constitutionally appellate jurisdiction under the judiciary act of 1789, ch. 20, sec. 25, from the final judgment or decree of the highest court of law or equity of a state having jurisdiction of the subject matter of the suit, where is drawn in question the validity of a treaty or statute of, or an authority exercised under the United States, and the decision is against their validity: or where is drawn in question the validity of a statute of, or an authority exercised under any state, on the ground of their being repugnant to the Constitution, treaties or laws of the United States, and the decision is in favour of such their validity: or of the Constitution, or of a treaty, or statute of, or commission held under the United States, and the decision is against the title, right, privilege, or exemption, specially set up or claimed by either party under such clause of the constitution, treaty, statute or commission. *Cohens* vs. *Virginia*, 6 *Wheaton*, 264. 375.

It is no objection to the exercise of this appellate jurisdiction, that one of the parties is a state, and the other a citizen of that state. *Ib.*

The Circuit Courts of the Union have chancery jurisdiction in every state: they have the same chancery powers, and the same rules of decision in equity cases in all the states. *United States* vs. *Howland*, 4 *Wheaton*, 108. 115.

Resolutions of the Legislature of Virginia of 1810, upon the proposition from Pennsylvania to amend the Constitution, so as to provide an impartial tribunal to decide disputes between the State and Federal Judiciaries. *Note to Cohens* vs. *Virginia*, Notes 6 *Wheaton*, 358.

Where a cause is brought to this Court by writ of error, or appeal from the highest court of law, or equity of a state, under the 25th section of the judiciary act of 1789, ch. 20, upon the ground that the validity of a statute of the United States was drawn in question, and that the decision of the state court was against its validity, &c. or that the validity ted ;[68] but when not committed within any State, the Trial shall be at such Place or

88. The object of this clause is, to secure to the

---

of the statute of a state was drawn in question as repugnant to the Constitution of the United States, and the decision was in favour of its validity, it must appear from the record, that the act of Congress, or the constitutionality of the state law was drawn in question. *Miller* vs. *Nicholls,* 4 *Wheaton,* 311, 315.

But it is not required that the record should in terms state a misconstruction of the act of Congress, or that it was drawn into question. It is sufficient to give this court jurisdiction of the cause, that the record should show that an act of Congress was applicable to the case. *Id.* 315.

The Supreme Court of the United States has no jurisdiction under the 25th section of the judiciary act of 1789, ch. 20, unless the judgment or decree of the state court be a final judgment or decree. A judgment reversing that of an inferior court, and awarding a *venire facias de novo,* is not a final judgment. *Houston* vs. *Moore,* 3 *Wheaton,* 433.

By the compact of 1802, settling the boundary line between Virginia and Tennessee, and the laws made in pursuance thereof, it is declared that all claims and titles to land derived from Virginia, or North Carolina, or Tennessee, which have fallen into the respective states, shall remain as secure to the owners thereof, as if derived from the Government within whose boundary they have fallen, and shall not be prejudiced or affected by the establishment of the line. Where the titles of both the plaintiff and defendant in ejectment were derived under grant from Virginia to lands which fell within the limits of Tennessee, it was held that a prior settlement right thereto which would in *equity* give the party a title, could not be asserted as a sufficient title in an action of ejectment brought in the Circuit Court of Tennessee,— *Robinson* vs. *Campbell,* 3 *Wheaton,* 212.

Although the State Courts of Tennessee have decided, that under their statutes (declaring an elder grant founded on a junior entry to be void) a junior patent to be founded on a prior entry shall prevail *at law* against a senior patent founded on a junior entry; this doctrine has never been extended beyond cases within the express provision of the statute of Tennessee, and could not apply to titles deriving all their validity from the laws of Virginia, and confirmed by the compact between the two states. *Id.* 212.

Places as the Congress may by Law have directed.*

SECTION 3. Treason against the United States, shall consist only in levying War against them, or in adhering to their Enemies, giving them aid and Comfort.[89]

party accused from being dragged to a trial in some distant state, away from his friends, and witnesses, and neighbourhood; and thus to be subjected to the verdict of mere strangers, who may feel no common sympathy, or who may even cherish animosities, or prejudices against him. Besides this, a trial in a distant state or territory might subject the party to the most oppressive expenses, or perhaps to the inability of procuring the proper witnesses to establish his innocence. There is little danger, indeed, that congress would ever exert their power in such an oppressive, and unjustifiable a manner. But upon a subject so vital to the security of the citizen, it was fit to leave as little as possible to mere discretion. By the common law, the trial of all crimes is required to be in the county, where they are committed. But as crimes may be committed on the high seas, and elsewhere, out of the territorial jurisdiction of a state, it was indispensable that, in such cases, congress should be enabled to provide the place of trial.—*Story's Com. v.* 3, *p.* 654, 655.

89. To constitute the specific crime "treason," war must be actually levied against the United States. However flagitious may be the crime of conspiring to subvert, by force, the government of our country, such conspiracy is not treason. It has

---

* See amendments, art. 6.

No person shall be convicted of Treason unless on the Testimony of two Witnesses to the same overt act, or on Confession in open Court.

The Congress shall have Power to declare the Punishment of Treason, but no Attainder of Treason shall work corruption of Blood or Forfeiture[90] except during the Life of the Person attainted.*

ARTICLE IV.

SECTION 1. Full Faith and Credit shall be given in each State to the public Acts,

---

been determined, that the actual enlistment of men to serve against the government does not amount to levying war. If, however, war be actually levied, all those who perform any part, however minute, and however remote from the scene of action, and who are actually leagued in the general conspiracy, are to be condemned as traitors. But there must be an actual assemblage of men for treasonable purposes, to constitute a levying of war.—*Story's Com. v. 3, p.* 670.

90. The punishment of treason is death by hanging. By corruption of blood according to the common law, all inheritable qualities are destroyed, so that an attainted person can neither inherit lands, nor other hereditaments from his ancestors, nor retain those he is already in possession of, nor transmit them to any heir.—*Story's Com. v.* 3, *p.* 171.

---

* See Laws of the U. States, vol. ii, ch. 36.

Records, and judicial Proceedings of every other State.*⁹¹ And the Congress may by general Laws prescribe the Manner in which such Acts, Records and Proceedings shall be proved, and the Effect thereof.

SECTION 2. The citizens of each State

91. It is well known that the laws and acts of foreign nations are not judicially taken notice of in any other nation; and that they must be proved, like any other facts, whenever they come into operation or examination in any forensic controversy.

As respects the several states here mentioned, it is intended that not only faith and credit to the public acts, records, and judicial proceedings of each of the states, such as belonged to those of all foreign nations and tribunals should be given; but also to give them *full* faith and credit; that is, to attribute to them positive and absolute verity, so that they cannot be contradicted, or the truth of them be denied, any more than in the state, where they originated.—*Story's Com. v.* 3, *p.* 175. 180.

(By an act of congress of the 26th of May,

---

* A judgment of a State Court has the same credit, validity and effect in every other court within the United States, which it had in the court where it was rendered; and whatever pleas would be good to a suit thereon in such state, and none others can be pleaded in any other court within the United States. *Hampton* vs. *McConnell*, 3 *Wheaton*, 234.

The record of a judgment in one state is conclusive evidence in another, although it appears that the suit in which it was rendered, was commenced by an attachment of property, the defendant having afterwards appeared and taken defence. *Mayhew* vs. *Thacher*, 6 *Wheaton*, 129.

shall be entitled to all Privileges and Immunities of Citizens in the several States.[92]

A Person charged in any State with Treason, Felony, or other Crime, who shall flee from Justice, and be found in another State, shall on Demand of the executive Authority of the State from which he fled, be delivered up, to be removed to the State having Jurisdiction of the Crime.

No Person held to Service or Labour in one

1790, (ch. 11.) the mode was prescribed of carrying into effect the objects of this clause.)—*Story's Com. v. 3, p.* 182.

92. This provision applies only to natural born or duly naturalized citizens, and if they remove from one state to another, they are entitled to the privileges that persons of the same description are entitled to in the state to which the removal is made, and to none other.—*Kent's Com. v.* 2, *p.* 71.

A citizen of Massachusetts would be entitled, in the State of New-York, to the same rights and privileges as a citizen of New-Jersey, or any other state; but neither could, without actually residing in the state a certain time, exercise *all* the rights of a citizen of the State of New-York. Such for instance as voting at elections, exemption from imprisonment for debt, and the like.

A state has a right to confer certain privileges upon its own citizens, and deny the same to citizens of other states; as for example, the Supreme Court have decided that a law of the State of New-Jersey, giving its own citizens the exclusive right of taking oysters within its chartered limits, was an exercise of a constitutional right possessed by the state.—*Compiler.*

State, under the Laws thereof, escaping into another, shall, in Consequence of any Law or Regulation therein, be discharged from such Service or Labour, but shall be delivered up on Claim of the Party to whom such Service or Labour may be due.[93]

SECTION 3. New States may be admitted by the Congress into this Union; but no new State shall be formed or erected within the Jurisdiction of any other State; nor any State be formed by the Junction of two or more States, or Parts of States, without the Consent of the Legislatures of the States concerned as well as of the Congress.

The Congress shall have Power to dispose of and make all needful Rules and Regulations respecting the Territory or other Property belonging to the United States; and nothing in this Constitution shall be so construed as to prejudice any Claims of the United States, or of any particular State.[94]

---

93. This clause was introduced into the constitution solely for the benefit of the slave holding states, to enable them to reclaim their fugitive slaves, who may have escaped into other states, where slavery is not tolerated.—*Story's Com. v.* 3, *p.* 676.

94. As the general government possesses the right to acquire territory, either by conquest or by treaty, it would seem to follow, as an inevitable consequence, that it possesses the power to govern what it has so acquired.

No one has ever doubted the authority of congress to erect territorial governments within the

SECTION 4. The United States shall guarantee to every State in this Union, a Republican Form of Government, and shall protect each of them against Invasion;[95] and on Application of the Legislature, or of the Executive (when the Legislature cannot be convened) against domestic Violence.

ARTICLE V.

The Congress, whenever two-thirds of both Houses shall deem it necessary, shall propose Amendments to this Constitution, or, on the Application of the Legislatures of two-thirds of

---

territory of the United States, under the general language of the clause. "to make all needful rules and regulations."—*Story's Com. v. 3, p.* 194, 195.

95. Whenever the states may choose to substitute other republican forms of government, they have a right to do so, and to claim the federal guaranty for the latter. The only restriction imposed on them is, that they shall not exchange republican for anti-republican constitutions; a restriction, which, it is presumed, will hardly be considered a grievance.

Protection against invasion is due from every society to the parts composing it. The latitude of the expression here used, seems to secure each state not only against *foreign hostility*, but against *ambitious or vindictive* enterprises of its more powerful neighbours.

Protection against domestic violence is added with equal propriety.—*Story's Com. v. 3, p.* 681, 682.

the several States, shall call a Convention for proposing Amendments, which, in either Case, shall be valid to all Intents and Purposes, as Part of this Constitution, when ratified by the Legislatures of three-fourths of the several States, or by Conventions in three fourths thereof, as the one or the other Mode of Ratification may be proposed by the Congress;[96] provided that no Amendment which may be made prior to the Year one thousand eight hundred and eight shall in any Manner affect the first and fourth Clauses in the Ninth Section of the first Article; and that no state, without its Consent, shall be deprived of its equal Suffrage in the Senate.*

ARTICLE VI.

All Debts contracted and Engagements entered into, before the Adoption of this Constitution, shall be as valid against the United States under this Constitution, as under the Confederation.[97]

96. A government, forever changing and changeable, is indeed, in a state bordering upon anarchy and confusion. A government, which, in its own organization, provides no means of change, but assumes to be fixed and unalterable, must, after a while, become wholly unsuited to the circumstances of the nation; and it will either degenerate into a despotism, or, by the pressure of its inequalities, bring on a revolution.—*Story's Com. v. 3, p. 686.*

97. Nothing is more clear upon reason or general

---

* See ante art. 1, sec. 3, clause 1.

This Constitution, and the Laws of the United States which shall be made in Pursuance thereof; and all Treaties made, or which shall be made, under the Authority of the United States, shall be the Supreme Law of the Land;*⁹⁸ and the Judges in every State shall

law, than the doctrine, that revolutions in government have, or ought to have, no effect whatsoever upon private rights, and contracts, or upon the public obligations of nations.—*Story's Com. v. 3, p.* 691.

98. The propriety of this clause would seem to result from the very nature of the constitution. If it was to establish a national government, that government ought, to the extent of its powers and rights, to be supreme. It would be a perfect solecism to affirm, that a national government should exist with certain powers; and yet, that in the exercise of those powers, it should not be supreme.

If a number of political societies enter into a larger political society, the laws, which the latter may enact, pursuant to the powers intrusted to it by its constitution, must necessarily be supreme over those societies, and the individuals of whom they are composed. It would otherwise be a mere treaty, dependent upon the good faith of the parties, and not a government, which is only another name for political power and supremacy. But it will not follow, that acts of the larger society, which are not pursuant to its constitutional powers, but

---

* An act of Congress repugnant to the Constitution cannot become a law. *Marbury* vs. *Madison*, 1 *Cranch*, 176.

be bound thereby, any Thing in the Constitution or Laws of any State to the Contrary notwithstanding.*

The Senators and Representatives before mentioned, and the Members of the several State Legislatures, and all executive and judicial Officers, both of the United States and of the several States, shall be bound by Oath or Affirmation, to support this Constitution,† but

which are invasions of the residuary authorities of the smaller societies, will become the supreme law of the land. They will be merely acts of usurpation, and will deserve to be treated as such.

From the supremacy of the constitution and laws and treaties of the United States, within their constitutional scope, arises the duty of courts of justice to declare any unconstitutional law passed by congress or by a state legislature, void. But the judiciary of the United States has no general jurisdiction to declare acts of the several states void, unless they are repugnant to the constitution of the United States, notwithstanding they are repugnant to the state constitutions.—*Story's Com. v. 3, p.* 698, 696. 701.

---

* The Courts of the United States are bound to take notice of the Constitution. *Marbury* vs. *Madison*, 1 *Cranch*, 178.

A contemporary exposition of the constitution practiced and acquiesced under for a period of years, fixes its construction. *Stuart* vs. *Laird*, 1 *Cranch*, 299.

The Government of the Union, though limited in its powers, is supreme within its sphere of action, and its laws when made in pursuance of the Constitution form the supreme law of the land. *McCulloch* vs. *State of Maryland*, 4 *Wheaton*, 405.

† See Laws of the United States, vol. ii, ch. 1.

no religious Test shall ever be required as a qualification to any Office or public Trust under the United States."

99. That all those, who are intrusted with the execution of the powers of the national government, should be bound by some solemn obligation to the due execution of the trust reposed in them, and to support the constitution, would seem to be a proposition too clear to render any reasoning necessary in support of it. Oaths have a solemn obligation upon the minds of all reflecting men, and especially upon those, who feel a deep sense of accountability to a supreme being.

The remaining part of the clause in relation " to any religious test," is not introduced merely for the purpose of satisfying the scruples of many respectable persons, who feel an invincible repugnance to any religious test, or affirmation. It had a higher object; to cut off for ever, every pretence of any alliance between church and state in the national government,—*Story's Com. v.* 3, *p.* 702, 705.

ARTICLE VII.

The Ratification of the Conventions of nine States, shall be sufficient for the Establishment of this Constitution between the States so ratifying the same.

Done in Convention by the Unanimous Consent of the States Present, the Seventeenth Day of September, in the Year of our Lord one thousand seven hundred and eighty-seven and of the Independence of the United States of America the Twelfth. In Witness whereof We have hereunto subscribed our Names.

GEO. WASHINGTON, *Presidt.*
and deputy from Virginia.

Attest,
William Jackson, *Secretary.*

New-Hampshire.
John Langdon,
Nicholas Gilman.
Massachusetts.
Nathaniel Gorham,
Rufus King.
Connecticut.
William Samuel Johnson,
Roger Sherman.
New-York.
Alexander Hamilton.
New-Jersey.
William Livingston,
David Brearly,
William Patterson,
Jonathan Dayton.
Pennsylvania.
Benjamin Franklin,
Thomas Mifflin,
Robert Morris,
George Clymer,
Thomas Fitzsimons,
Jared Ingersoll,
James Wilson,
Gouverneur Morris.
Delaware.
George Read,
Cunning Bedford, junr.
John Dickinson,
Richard Bassett,
Jacob Broom.
Maryland.
James M'Henry,
Dan. of St. Thomas Jenifer,
Daniel Carroll.
Virginia.
John Blair,
James Madison, junr.
North Carolina.
William Blount,
Richard Dobbs Spaight,
Hugh Williamson.

South Carolina.
John Rutledge,
Charles Cotesworth Pinckney,
Charles Pinckney,
Pierce Butler.

Georgia.
William Few,
Abraham Baldwin.

☞ Congress at its first session, begun and held in the City of New-York, on Wednesday, the 4th of March, 1789, proposed to the Legislatures of the several States, twelve amendments to the Constitution, ten of which, only, were adopted. They are the ten first following.

AMENDMENTS[100]

To the Constitution of the United States, ratified according to the provisions of the Vth Article of the foregoing Constitution.

ARTICLE THE FIRST. Congress shall make no Law respecting an establishment of Religion, or prohibiting the free exercise thereof;[101] or

Amendments.

100. The amendments to the constitution are generally principles similar to those incorporated in some of our state constitutions, denominated, "bill of rights."

101. The first is that congress shall make no law respecting "an establishment of religion."
It was under a solemn consciousness of the dangers from ecclesiastical ambition, the bigotry of spiritual pride, and the intolerance of sects, thus exemplified in our domestic, as well as in foreign annals, that it was deemed advisable to exclude from the national government all power to act upon the subject.—*Story's Com. v.* 3, *p.* 730.
The same principle recognised in the constitution of the United States in relation "to an establishment of religion," generally pervades the

abridging the freedom of Speech, or of the Press;[102] or the right of the People peaceably

constitutions of the several states. All religious sects are tolerated; all are placed on the same footing as other citizens; and all are equally protected in the exercise of their religious opinions; and it is firmly believed, that wherever this equality, and these rights and privileges prevail, the sublime doctrines of christianity, under truly pious and devoted teachers, cannot but flourish. The question is sometimes agitated as to the extent, that the christian religion is binding, not in an exclusively *moral*, but also in a *political* point of view. In order to a clear and full understanding of this question, it may be proper to observe, that man is accountable, to a certain extent, for his actions, to human government; and in the second place, that he is accountable to his God, *for all his actions*. Human society has found it necessary to incorporate a part of the decalogue in its civil jurisprudence; such for instance, as "thou shalt not kill, thou shalt not steal," &c. These, to all intents and purposes are *politically binding*. Other parts of the decalogue, such for instance as "thou shalt not covet thy neighbours house," &c., are not, and from the very nature of the case, cannot, be politically binding; it is an exclusive act of the mind which no human tribunal could reach. It is moreover an act for which man is accountable only to his God: and any human legislative, or judicial action upon a subject of this nature, would, in the opinion of the compiler, be the height of blasphemy.— *Compiler.*

Freedom of speech or of the press.

102. That this amendment was intended to secure

to every citizen an absolute right to speak, or write, or print, whatever he might please, without any responsibility, public or private, therefore is a supposition too wild to be indulged by any rational man. This would be to allow to every citizen a right to destroy, at his pleasure, the reputation, the peace, the property, and even the personal safety of every other citizen. A man might out of mere malice and revenge, accuse another of the most infamous crimes; might excite against him the indignation of all his fellow citizens by the most atrocious calumnies; might disturb, nay, overturn all his domestic peace, and embitter all his parental affections; civil society could not go on under such circumstances. Men would then be obliged to resort to private vengeance, to make up for the deficiencies of the law; and assassinations and savage cruelties would be perpetrated with all the frequency belonging to barbarous and brutal communities.

It is neither more nor less, than an expansion of the great doctrine, recently brought into operation in the law of libel, that every man shall be at liberty to publish what is true, with good motives and for justifiable ends. And with this reasonable limitation it is not only right in itself, but it is an estimable privilege in a free government.—*Story's Com. v. 3, p. 731, 732.*

Libel.

A libel, as defined by General Hamilton, and since recognised by the Supreme Court of the state of New-York, " is a censorious or ridiculing writing, picture, or sign; made with a mischievous or malicious intent, towards government, magistrates, or individuals." The author of a libel against an individual is liable to two prosecutions; one in *a civil action for damages*, by the person libelled; the other, in *a public prosecution by way of indictment*.

In a *civil action*, it is in all cases, a sufficient justification to prove the truth of the publication charged as libellous.

A *public prosecution* is a question of state policy; and by the English common law, according to the opinion of some, the truth of the matter charged in an indictment as libellous, is no justification; and so late as 1804, two out of four judges of the Supreme Court of the state of New-York, in the case of *The People* v. *Croswell*, gave as their opinion, that the truth was not a justification. The Supreme Court, when full, consisted of five judges; but at the time of this trial, there were but four on the bench; Lewis, (since Governor of the state) and Livingston, (late one of the justices of the Supreme Court) were of opinion that the truth was no justification. Thompson, (one of the present justices of the Supreme Court) and Kent, (late Chancellor of the state of New-York) were of opinion that the truth of a libel ought to be given in evidence, and that it ought to be a justification, provided that it appeared on the trial, that the matter charged as libellous, was published with good motives, and for justifiable ends."

The opinion of the two judges first named, is said to have been predicated upon a clause contained in the thirty-fifth article of the first constitution of the state of New-York, which declared, " That such parts of the common law of England, and of the statute law of England and Great Britain, and of the acts of the legislature of the colony of New-York, as together did form the law of the said colony on the 19th day of April, in the year of our Lord one thousand seven hundred and seventy-five, shall be and continue the law of this state, subject to such alterations and provisions as the legislature of this state shall, from time to time, make concerning the same."

This division of opinion in the Supreme Court led, during the year 1804–5, to an act of the legislature of the state of New-York, in which it was declared, that the truth shall, in all cases, on an indictment for a libel, be a justification; provided, that it appear that " the matter charged as libellous was published from good motives, and for justifiable ends." The same provision is contained in the eighth section of the seventh article of the new constitution of the state of New-York, which was adopted in the year 1822.

The framers of that instrument wisely limited the justification on an indictment for a libel, not to the *truth* of the matter charged as libellous, but to such publications, as, in the opinion of the jury, were made "*from good motives, and for justifiable ends.*" Were it not for this provision, the peace of society might be continually disturbed with impunity. The most abandoned and unprincipled, under the mask of publishing the truth, might, from the very worst of motives, and without rendering any good to the public, destroy the peace of our most valuable citizens. A person might be held up to ridicule, and his feelings tortured, on account of some stain upon the character of his family connexions; he may, through actual and unavoidable misfortunes, have descended from a state of affluence, to that of extreme poverty; or, he may have become deformed, or received some other affliction of Providence, over which he could have no control. In all such cases as these, it is believed that an honest and intelligent jury would decide, " that the *greater the truth, the greater the libel*," and that the court would award the punishment accordingly.

On the other hand, suppose a person were a notorious swindler or hypocrite; or were guilty of practices calculated to deceive, impose upon, or injure the community—*all* these, and similar ones, to assemble, and to petition the Government for a Redress of grievances.[103]

ARTICLE THE SECOND. A well regulated Militia, being necessary to the security of a free

are cases in which the best interests of community are concerned, and the jury would have a right to infer good motives, from the very act itself, in the publisher who should be the means of putting the community on their guard against such persons.—*Compiler.*

Right of petition.

103. It is impossible, that this privilege (even if it were not expressly secured to the people) could be practically denied, until the spirit of liberty had wholly disappeared, and the people had become so servile and debased, as to be unfit to exercise any of the privileges of freemen.—*Story's Com. v. 3, p.* 745.

To petition government, is the inherent right of a free people. It is not the *right*, but the *duty* of rulers to respectfully hear and determine all lawful applications from the people. No matter if those intrusted with legislation are opposed to a measure asked for, the petitioners are to be no less civilly or respectfully treated on that account; and should the time ever arrive, when we shall witness a member of the senate, or of the house of representatives, so far degrade himself, as to treat the petition or petitioners for any lawful measure, in any other way than with the most profound respect, it will clearly indicate an abandonment, or an original want of principle, of gentlemanly deportment, and of self-respect; and, in most cases, a degraded class of constituents.—*Compiler.*

State, the right of the people to keep and bear Arms, shall not be infringed.[104]

ARTICLE THE THIRD. No Soldier shall, in time of peace, be quartered in any house, without the consent of the Owner, nor in time of war, but in a manner to be prescribed by law.[105]

ARTICLE THE FOURTH. The right of the People to be secure in their persons, houses, papers, and effects, against unreasonable searches and seizures, shall not be violated, and no warrants shall issue, but upon probable cause, supported by Oath or Affirmation, and particularly describing the place to be searched, and the persons or things to be seized.[106]

104. The militia is the natural defence of a free country against sudden foreign invasions, domestic insurrections, and domestic usurpations of power by rulers.

The right of the citizen to keep and bear arms has justly been considered, as the palladium of the liberties of a republic; since it offers a strong moral check against the usurpation and arbitrary power of rulers; and will generally, even if these are successful in the first instance, enable the people to resist and triumph over them.—*Story's Com. v. 3, p.* 746.

105. This privilege speaks for itself. Its plain object is to secure the perfect enjoyment of that great right of the common law, that a man's house shall be his own castle, privileged against all civil and military intrusion.—*Story's Com. v. 3, p.* 747.

106. This provision seems indispensable to the full enjoyment of the rights of personal security, personal liberty, and private property. It is little more than the affirmance of a great constitutional

ARTICLE THE FIFTH. No person shall be held to answer for a capital, or otherwise infamous crime, unless on a presentment or indictment of a Grand Jury, except in cases arising in the land or naval forces, or in the Militia, when in actual service in time of war or public danger;[107]

doctrine of the common law. And its introduction into the amendments was doubtless occasioned by the strong sensibility excited both in England and America, upon the subject of general warrants, almost upon the eve of the American revolution. A warrant, and the complaint on which the same is founded, to be legal, must not only state the name of the party, but also the time, and place, and nature of the offence with reasonable certainty. *Story's Com. v. 3, p.* 748. 750.

Considering with what scrupulous nicety the constitution protects the rights of persons suspected of having committed an offence, it certainly cannot be unreasonable to suppose, but that the same protection should be given to a person, as to his papers, when required in an investigation of a civil nature; it also seems to be reasonable, that no person should be required to submit his books, papers, &c., to an investigation in a civil suit, except in the presence of the owner, agent, or trustee.—*Compiler.*

107. It is obvious that the grand jury perform most important public functions; and are a great security to citizens against vindictive prosecutions, either by the government, or by political partizans, or by private enemies. Nor is this all; the indictment must charge the time, and place, and nature, and circumstances of the offence with clearness and certainty; so that the party may have full notice of the charge, and be able to make his defence with all reasonable knowledge and ability.—*Story's Com. v. 3, p.* 658.

nor shall any person be subject for the same offence to be twice put in jeopardy of life or limb ;[108] nor shall be compelled in any criminal case to be a witness against himself, nor be deprived of life, liberty, or property, without due process of law ;[109] nor shall private property be taken for public use, without just compensation.[110]

"*Shall not be put twice in jeopardy for the same offence.*"

108. This is a great privilege secured by the common law. The meaning of it is, that a party shall not be *tried* a second time for the same offence, after he has once been convicted or acquitted of the offence charged, by the verdict of a jury, and a judgment has passed thereon for or against him. But it does not mean, that he shall not be tried for the offence a second time, if the jury have been discharged without giving any verdict; or, if, having given a verdict, judgment has been arrested upon it, or a new trial has been granted in his favour; for, in such a case, his life or limb cannot be judicially said to have been put in jeopardy.—*Story's Com. v.* 3, *p.* 659.

" *No person in a criminal case to be a witness against himself.*"

109. This also is but an affirmance of a common law privilege. But it is of inestimable value. It is well known, that in some countries, not only are criminals compelled to give evidence against themselves, but are subjected to the rack or torture in order to procure a confession of guilt.—*Story's Com. v.* 3, *p.* 660.

"*Private property for public use.*"

110. This is an affirmance of a great doctrine

ARTICLE THE SIXTH. In all criminal prosecutions, the accused shall enjoy the right to a speedy and public trial, by an impartial jury of the State and District wherein the Crime shall have been committed, which district shall have been previously ascertained by law, and to be informed of the Nature and Cause of the accusation; to be confronted with the Witnesses against him; to have compulsory process for obtaining Witnesses in his favour, and to have the Assistance of Counsel for his defence.

ARTICLE THE SEVENTH. In suits at common law, where the value in controversy shall exceed twenty dollars, the right of trial by Jury, shall be preserved,[111] and no fact tried by a Jury, established by the common law for the protection of private property.

The provisions of the fifth and sixth articles secure the people a constitutional right on points which the common law had in some cases left in a doubtful and questionable state.—*Story's Com. v. 3, p.* 658, 659, 660, 661.

111. One of the strongest objections, originally taken by the people against the constitution of the United States, was the want of an express provision securing the right of trial by jury in civil cases, and this amendment was proposed to allay their fears and jealousies upon that point.

The amendment was universally approved of, and was considered as the establishment of a fundamental guaranty of the rights and liberties of the people.

The phrase "common law," found in this clause, is used in contradistinction to equity, and admiralty, and maritime jurisprudence.

shall be otherwise re-examined in any Court of the United States, than according to the rules of the common law.*[112]

It is well known, that in civil causes, in courts of equity and admiralty, juries do not intervene; and that courts of equity use the trial by jury only in extraordinary cases to inform the conscience of the court. When, therefore, we find that the amendment requires, that the right of trial by jury shall be preserved in suits "at common law," the natural conclusion is, that this distinction was present to the minds of the framers of the constitution. By "*common law*," they meant, what the constitution denominated in the third article " law;" not merely suits which the *common law* recognised among its old and settled proceedings, but suits, in which *legal* rights were to be ascertained and determined, in contradistinction to those, in which equitable rights alone were recognised, and equitable remedies were administered; or in which, as in the admiralty, a mixture of public law, and of maritime law and equity, was often found in the same suit.

112. But the other clause of the amendment is still more important; and we read it, as a substan-

---

* The act of assembly of Maryland, of 1793, ch. 30, incorporating the Bank of Columbia, and giving to the Corporation a summary process by execution in the nature of an attachment against its debtors who have by an express consent in writing, made the bonds, bills or notes by them drawn or endorsed negotiable at the Bank, is not repugnant to the Constitution of the United States or of Maryland. *Bank of Columbia* vs. *Okely*, 4 *Wheaton*, 236. 249.

But the last provision in the act of incorporation which gives this summary process to the Bank, is no part of its corporate franchise, and may be repealed or altered at pleasure by the legislative will, *Id.* 245.

ARTICLE THE EIGHTH. Excessive bail shall not be required, nor excessive fines imposed, nor cruel and unusual punishments inflicted.[113]

ARTICLE THE NINTH. The enumeration in the Constitution, of certain rights, shall not be construed to deny or disparage others retained by the people.[114]

tial and independent clause. "No fact tried by a jury shall be otherwise re-examinable, in any courts of the United States, than according to the rules of the common law." This is a prohibition to the courts of the United States to re-examine any facts tried by a jury in any other manner. The only modes known to the common law to re-examine such facts, are the granting a new trial by the court, where the issue was tried, or to which the record was properly returnable; or the award of a venire facias de novo, by an appellate court, for some error of law, which intervened in the proceedings.—*Story's Com. v. 3, p. 641, 642. 644. 647.*

113. This provision would seem to be wholly unnecessary in a free government, since it is scarcely possible, that any department of such a government should authorize or justify such atrocious conduct.

It has been held in the state courts, (and the point does not seem ever to have arisen in the courts of the United States) that this clause does not apply to punishments inflicted in a state court for a crime against such state; but that the prohibition is addressed solely to the national government, and operates as a restriction upon its powers.—*Story's Com. v. 3, p. 751.*

114. This clause was manifestly introduced to prevent any perverse or ingenious misapplication of the well known maxim, that an affirmation in

138

ARTICLE THE TENTH. The Powers not delegated to the United States, by the Constitution, nor prohibited by it to the States, are reserved to the States respectively, or to the people.*[115]

particular cases implies a negation in all others; and é converso that a negation in particular cases implies an affirmation in all others. The maxim, rightly understood, is perfectly sound and safe; but it has often been strangely forced from its natural meaning into the support of the most dangerous political heresies.—*Story's Com. v.* 8, *p.* 752.

115. This amendment is a mere affirmation of

---

* The powers granted to Congress are not exclusive of similar powers existing in the States, unless where the Constitution has expressly in terms given an exclusive power to Congress, or the exercise of a like power is prohibited to the States, or there is a direct repugnancy or incompatibility in the exercise of it by the States. *Houston* vs. *Moore*, 5 *Wheaton*, 1. 12.

The example of the first class is to be found in the exclusive legislation delegated to Congress over places purchased by the consent of the Legislature of the State in which the same shall be for forts, arsenals, dock-yards, &c. Of the second class, the prohibition of a State to coin money, or emit bills of credit. Of the third class, the power to establish an uniform rule of naturalization, and the delegation of admiralty and maritime jurisdiction. *Ib.* 49.

In all other classes of cases, the States retain concurrent authority with Congress. *Id.* 49.

But in cases of concurrent authority where the laws of the States and the Union are in direct and manifest collision on the same subject, those of the Union being the supreme law of the land are of paramount authority, and the State laws so far, and so far only as such incompatibility exists, must necessarily yield. *Id.* 49.

There is nothing in the Constitution of the United States similar to the articles of confederation, which excludes inci-

ARTICLE THE ELEVENTH.* The judicial power of the United States shall not be construed to extend to any suit in law or equity, commenced or prosecuted against one of the United States by Citizens of another State, or by Citizens or Subjects of any foreign State.[116]

what, upon any just reasoning, is a necessary rule of interpreting the constitution. Being an instrument of limited and enumerated powers, it follows irresistibly, that what *is not conferred, is withheld*, and belongs to the state authorities, if invested by their constitutions of government respectively in them; and if not so invested, it is retained by the people, as a part of their residuary sovereignty.—*Story's Com. v.* 3, *p.* 752.

116. Before the adoption of this article, an important constitutional question became the subject of litigation, involving the question whether the jurisdiction given by the constitution in cases in in which a *state* is a party, extended to suits brought

---

dental or implied powers. *McCulloch* vs. *State of Maryland*, 4 *Wheaton*, 406.

If the *end* be legitimate and within the scope of the Constitution, all the *means* which are appropriate, which are plainly adapted to that end, and which are not prohibited, may constitutionally be employed to carry it into effect. *Id.* 421.

The act of Congress of 4th May, 1812, entitled "An act further to amend the charter of the city of Washington," which provides (sec. 6) that the corporation of the city shall be empowered for certain purposes and under certain restrictions, to authorize the drawing of lotteries, does not extend to authorize the corporation to force the sale of the tickets in such lottery, in States where such sale may be prohibited by the State laws. *Cohens* vs. *Virginia*, 6 *Wheaton*, 264. 375.

* This amendment was proposed at the first session of the third Congress. See ante art. 3, sec. 2, clause 1.

against a state, as well as *by* it, or was exclusively confined to the latter. The question was made, and most elaborately considered in the celebrated case of *Ghisholm* v. *Georgia*, (see 2d Dallas' Reports, p. 474;) and the majority of the Supreme Court held, that the judicial power under the constitution applied equally to suits brought by, and against a state. At the time when this decision was made, many suits were pending against several of the states; the decision created great alarm among the states, on account of their liability to be frequently harrassed for claims that might be brought against them. An amendment was consequently proposed, and ratified by the states, by which the power was entirely taken away, so far as it regards suits brought *against* a state. This amendment was so construed as to include suits *then pending*, as well as suits *to be commenced* thereafter; and accordingly all the suits then pending *were* dismissed, without any further adjudication.

Decisions.

The Supreme Court have decided that the amendment applies only to *original suits against a state;* and does not touch the appellate jurisdiction of the Supreme Court to re-examine, on an appeal or writ of error, a judgment or decree rendered in any state court, in a suit brought originally *by a state* against any private person.

When is a state a party to a suit?

A state, in the sense of the constitution, is a party only, when it is on the record as such; and it *sues,* or *is sued* in its political capacity.

It is not sufficient, that it may have an interest in a suit between other persons, or that its rights, powers, privileges, or duties, come therein incidentally in question. It must *be in terms a plaintiff* or *defendant*, so that the judgment or decree may be binding upon it, as it is in common suits binding upon parties and privies.

It is, moreover, not sufficient, that the state may have an interest in the cause, or that the parties before the court are sued for acts done, as agents of the state. The same principle applies to cases where a state has an interest in a corporation; as when it is a stockholder in an incorporated bank or other institution; the corporation is still suable, although the state, as such, is exempted from any action.— *Story's Com. v. 3, p.* 547, 548, 549, 550.

For article the twelfth, see page 67.*

[Before bringing this work to a close, the compiler has thought proper to introduce to the reader, and to recommend to his serious consideration, the following extract, from the Commentaries, of that profound jurist, and accomplished scholar, Judge Story.]

In taking a survey of our admirable constitution, the learned commentator goes on to say:

"Yet, after all, the fabric may fall; for the work of man is perishable, and must for ever have inherent elements of decay! Nay, it *must perish*, if

---

☞ *Note.* Another amendment was proposed as Article xiii, at the second session of the eleventh Congress, but not having been ratified by a sufficient number of States, has not yet become valid as a part of the Constitution of the United States. It is erroneously given as a part of the Constitution, in page 74, vol. i, Laws of the United States.

there be not that vital spirit in the people, which alone can nourish, sustain, and direct all its movements. It is in vain, that statesmen shall form plans of government, in which the beauty and harmony of a republic shall be embodied in visible order, shall be built up on solid substructions, and adorned by every useful ornament, if the inhabitants suffer the silent power of time to dilapidate its walls, or crumble its massy supporters into dust; if the assaults from *without* are never resisted, and the rottenness and mining from *within* are never guarded against. Who can preserve the rights and liberties of the people, when they shall be abandoned by themselves? Who shall keep watch in the temple, when the watchmen sleep at their posts? Who shall call upon the people to redeem their possessions, and revive the republic, when their own hands have deliberately and corruptly surrendered them to the oppressor, and have built the prisons, or dug the graves of their own friends? This dark picture, it is to be hoped, will never be applicable to the republic of America. And yet it affords a warning, which, like all the lessons of past experience, we are not permitted to disregard. America, free, happy, and enlightened, as she is, must rest the preservation of her rights and liberties upon the virtue, independence, justice, and sagacity of the people. If either fail, the republic is gone. Its *shadow* may remain with all the pomp, and circumstance, and trickery of government, but its *vital power* will have departed. In America, the demagogue may arise, as well as elsewhere. He is the natural, though spurious growth of republics; and, like the courtier, he may, by his blandishments, delude the ears and blind the eyes of the people to their own destruction. If ever the day shall arrive, in which the best talents and the best virtues shall be driven from office by intrigue or corruption, by the ostracism of the press, or the still more unrelenting persecution of party, legislation will cease to be national. It will be *wise* by accident, and *bad* by system."—*Story's Com. v. 2, p.* 364, 365.

I have examined and compared the foregoing print of the Constitution of the United States, and the amendments thereto, for the National Calendar of 1828, with the rolls in this office, and find it a faithful and literal copy of the said Constitution and amendments, in the text and punctuation thereof.—It appears that the ten first amendments, which were proposed at the first session of the First Congress of the United States, were finally ratified by the Constitutional number of States, on the fifteenth day of December, 1791; that the eleventh amendment, which was proposed at the first session of the Third Congress, was declared, in a message from the President of the United States to both Houses of Congress, dated 8th January, 1798, to have been adopted by three-fourths, the Constitutional number of States; and that the twelfth amendment, which was proposed at the first session of the Eighth Congress, was adopted by three fourths, the Constitutional number of States, in the year one thousand eight hundred and four, according to a public notice thereof, by the Secretary of State, under date the 25th of September, of the same year.

DANIEL BRENT, *Chief Clerk.*

Department of State, Washington, 25th Feb., 1828.

INDEX.

A.
	PAGE
Adjournment powers of each House	16
Amendments to the Constitution	120

B.
Bills for raising revenue.............................. 19

C.
Constitution and laws of U. S., Supreme law of the land. 122
Congress, powers of.....................................
  .. to lay taxes, duties, and imposts, provide for
the common defence and general welfare............ 21
  .. borrow money.............................. 28
  .. regulate commerce, &c...................... 28
  .. establishment of naturalization............. 29
  .. coin money, &c............................ 31
  .. provide for the punishment of counterfeiting
securities.. 33
  .. establish post offices and post roads......... 33
  .. promote the progress of science............. 34
  .. constitute tribunals inferior to the Supreme
Court... 35
  .. define and punish piracies................... 35
  .. declare war, &c............................ 36
  .. raise and support armies................... 37
  .. provide for calling forth the militia......... 38
  .. organizing and disciplining the army........ 39
  .. exclusive legislation in places 10 miles square 39

	PAGE
Congress to make all laws necessary to carry into effect the delegated powers	41
.. to dispose of and make rules respecting territory	
.. under which head is purchase of foreign territory	46
.. embargoes	47
.. priority of debts due the United States	48
Congress prohibitions:	
.. .. Writ of habeas corpus	49
.. .. bill of attainder on ex post facto laws	50
.. .. capitation or direct tax	50
.. .. duty on articles exported from any state	51
.. .. preference of trade	51
.. .. money drawn from the treasury	51
.. .. title of nobility by U. States or any state	52
.. .. treaty by any state	52
.. .. emit bills of credit, make any thing but gold a legal tender, or any law impairing the obligation of a contract	53
.. .. make no law respecting religion, or abridging freedom of speech or press	126

D.

Debts of the United States	121

E.

Elections for senators and representatives	16
Executive power	60
Elections of President and Vice President	60

I.

Impeachment	15
Judiciary	100
.. Supreme Court	100
(Inferior) Circuit and District	101
.. suits at common law shall not be construed to extend to suits against any one of the States	139

L.

	PAGE
Legislative power, House of Representatives and Senate	2
Libel	129

O.

Oaths of office	67

P.

President, powers and duties of	67, 90
.. powers of, to make treaties	69
.. nominate and appoint	69
.. his protest, review of	9

R.

Representatives of the House, composed of	2
.. age of members	2
Representative and direct taxes, appointment of	3
.. House choose their speaker	5
Rights of the people	132
.. states	138

S.

Senators, how chosen, and for what time	5
.. age of, to be eligible	7
Senate, President of and other officers	8
.. powers of to try impeachment	8
States, full faith and credit to its proceedings	116
.. prohibitions to form treaties, coin money, emit bills of credit, &c	52
.. new states	119

T.

Trials by jury	112
Treason, definition of, and punishment	115

V.

Vacancies, House of Representatives, how supplied	5

ERRATA.

Page 78, line 10, for *it is*, read *they are*.
.. 78, line 16, for *might*, read *would*.

www.ingramcontent.com/pod-product-compliance
Lightning Source LLC
Chambersburg PA
CBHW031458160426
43195CB00010BB/1019